HOW TO PLAY THE
GUITAR

HOW TO PLAY THE
GUITAR

Reading music, Chord construction and Interpretation
for all styles of Guitar playing.

CHARTWELL BOOKS Inc.
New York

Acknowledgements

In the course of writing and compiling this book I met many truly talented and professional individuals who worked with me, with unstinting effort, towards the betterment of tutorial standards for the guitar. To them I offer my sincere thanks for their unselfish devotion and co-operation on behalf of the pupils who will benefit.

I would also like to extend deep gratitude to my immediate family, without whose support and reassurance my task would have been immeasurably greater.

I am grateful, too, to the Yamaha Corporation for their assistance.

Peter Collins

Published by Chartwell Books Inc.
A division of Book Sales Inc.
110 Enterprise Avenue,
Secaucus, New Jersey
ISBN 0 89009 055 6
Library of Congress
Catalog Card Number 75 45874
© Copyright Paul Hamlyn Pty. Limited, Australia 1976

CONTENTS

Introduction

This book has been arranged to suit three possible uses. First, as a self-tutor for those who want to teach themselves to play the guitar; second, as a supplementary tutor for use with other tutors, or for those who wish to complement what they learn from a teacher; and third, as a reference and textbook for more experienced players and teachers.

For far too long traditional guitar tutors have been published without sufficient space being devoted to text, thus stifling anyone anxious to obtain additional information about one aspect or another of guitar playing and music for the guitar. This book is therefore intended to programme the pupil so that necessary related knowledge about the guitar can be absorbed, simply and painlessly, from the first chapter. This knowledge is gradually broadened, as the book and the student progress, until such time as the student is capable of supplementing the introductory technicalities (if that is felt necessary) with the aid of other tutors. Thus, although you may find that the material supplied up to and including the sixth string is seemingly overwhelming, it is in fact designed to promote, methodically, an acute awareness of important aspects of the guitar at the most crucial time—when you are still impressionable and not locked into inflexible or bad habits. By the time you have mastered the first part of the book, which might take only a few months, you will be capable of playing the guitar well—and of sight-reading well, too. Needless to say, perseverance is essential.

The remainder of the book moves quickly, and has been specifically designed so that you may add and incorporate other carefully selected material from other sources, thus allowing you to develop and diversify in a style best suited to you. It should be added here that the book is not intended to change or replace the teaching style used by any teacher, but rather to supplement whatever system or tutor a teacher may favour. The Blues Supplement has been included in a manner that does not demand your being able to read music in order to reap the benefits that it promotes—but it does set out to remind you that music can be fun to learn.

PART ONE

Introducing the guitar

CHAPTER 1 A Brief History of the Guitar

The guitar emerges as an instrument of integrity

Although the guitar in its present form is a comparative newcomer as an 'acceptable' musical instrument, it is in fact among the most ancient instruments known to man. The protruding neck attached to a vibration box, which enhances controlled volume and tone, is one of the oldest forms of amplified sound production. Primitive instruments of this type are still used in parts of Africa, and are similar in concept to the single-string-and-soapbox double bass style instrument popular with American 'hillbilly' bands.

No single nation or culture can claim to have invented the guitar. Many peoples in many different regions created distinctive 'sound box' instruments that date back more than 2,000 years. The *kissar*, *kithara* and *lyre* developed in the Mediterranean area; the *nefer* originated in northern Africa; and the Chinese lay claim to one of the oldest of popular instruments, the *tze-tze*, a small box-like unit with a neck of bamboo and four strings, which has remained unaltered for 2,500 years.

Even older are guitar-like instruments depicted in Egyptian tomb carvings dating from about 2,000 BC. Deterioration of the carvings has made positive identification impossible and has led to many arguments as to whether these instruments, played by monks, can truly be included in the 'guitar-type' category.

The first fretted instruments appeared after the fall of the Roman Empire. They were known by the old Greek name *kithara*, from which 'guitar' and 'zither' have since evolved. The Roman equivalent of this instrument, the *fidula*, was fretless and more like the modern 'fiddle'.

Contrary to popular belief, the Spaniards were not introduced to stringed instruments until about AD 800 when Arab invaders brought with them many examples in various shapes and sizes. The Spaniards called the stringed instrument *vihuela*, derived from *kithara*; the Portuguese named it *violao*, a name still used today; and the French, after minor changes, settled on the name *chrotta* (or *crota*) for the instrument that became the forerunner of the modern guitar.

The *chrotta*, originally used only for accompaniments, was gradually refined and developed to produce harmonic vibrations of exacting quality that enabled it to be used as an instrument for solo performances. The foundations of the modern guitar were laid in Spain with the combining of the style of the newly refined *chrotta* and that of the then popular lute. This innovation made Spain the paramount nation in the development of the guitar as a recognised and respectable instrument, and the Spanish guitar gradually took precedent over the lute (almost causing its extinction) because of mellower tone involvements and simpler forms of fingering.

The seventeenth century saw the guitar growing in popularity throughout Europe at an incredible speed. At this time, too, an additional string (the sixth) was added, tuned two octaves apart from the first and thus increasing the range of the instrument to three and a half octaves. This extraordinary span, which could be fully employed at one time, gave birth to the concert classical guitar. The increased range and the upsurge in popularity demanded a larger sound box to enhance volume and improve concert hall production. The innovations also encouraged the transcription for the guitar of music previously written only for the organ or other instruments.

With its span of three and a half octaves (some modern versions have a range of four octaves) the guitar permits three separate patterns of expression—solo, rhythm and bass, all of which can be played simultaneously. There are no restrictions concerning the strings to which these forms can be applied, thus allowing the performer an enormous range of self-expression and an endless variety of tones.

The depth and quality of the guitar have not altered much in the past century and a half, and the instrument still enjoys the name 'Spanish guitar' due to its unusual method of tuning being similar to that of the old Spanish *vihuela*. The portability and versatility of the guitar, together with its unique and peculiar harmonies in sound production, have advanced its popularity immeasurably in the last fifty years. Even the novice will discover within a few hours that he can express his mood on an instrument that 'exceeds the versatility of the piano', and will quickly learn to apply himself to reproducing emotions through his hands.

The popular music of today relies heavily on the guitar. Its peculiar dominance as an instrument demands and holds the interest of the listener irrespective of whether it is being played brilliantly or not so brilliantly. In the hands of its most accomplished exponents—classical, jazz, blues, rock, and so on—it has become a superb solo instrument, and is increasingly regarded as an outstanding instrument in its own right (a far cry from the days not so long past when it was dismissed as fit for little more than accompaniments, simple melodies and occasional flashes of brilliance in the traditional Spanish style).

The long history of the guitar has been one of adaptation and survival. Many instruments have perished as music has progressed; others have changed radically from their original form; but the guitar, taking changes in its stride (though sometimes slow to adapt), has maintained its essential features while improving its capabilities. If any instrument can be described as possessing 'integrity', that instrument is the guitar. And if the introduction of the electronic music synthesiser might have seemed to spell doom for the guitar, it should be noted that the guitar itself (albeit with the aid of electronics) can maintain its form and still simulate the sound of the great simulator! It is, in fact, helping to pave the way for the new electronic marvel of music.

CHAPTER 2   # The Construction of a Guitar

The parts of a guitar

The construction of this seemingly simple instrument is more complex than appearances suggest. Approximately 80 pieces of various woods and 70 pieces of metals and plastics are used in the manufacture of an average instrument.

The guitar can be conveniently divided into three parts, each of which will be discussed separately.

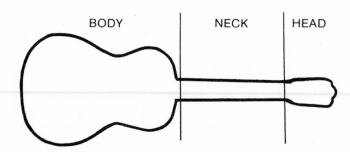

The body is made up of (a) the face, (b) the sides and (c) the back.

The FACE requires the greatest delicacy in construction. Although its hourglass shape looks simple, a great deal of work is involved on its underside.

The texture, grain and formation of the woods used in the face can make or break it and can, in turn, make or break the guitar. The wood graining must be fine, straight and narrow, without blemishes, knots or warps. The straight-faced grain permits an even distribution of sound and therefore enhances the tonal 'colour' of the guitar. It follows that the selection of woods is vital.

However, a revolutionary process of 'molecular bombardment' recently developed in Australia enables the quality of inferior woods to be improved. The wood is placed in an electronic mould and bombarded by as many as 3,000 molecules per second for up to ten hours. This bombardment simulates two hundred years of aging by natural processes. Crooked grains are straightened, imperfections disappear and even bad knots are reduced to barely visible minor blemishes.

The internal bracing applied to the underside of the face is as important (if not more so) as the construction and graining of the face. The four bracing methods illustrated here rely on different concepts to produce the styles that are characteristic of different types of guitars. The combination of graining and bracing determines the sound output. The bracing collects the tone being released from the bridge, locks its position, and then guides it along the grains until it is deflected through the last brace in the sound-hole area.

(1) FAN BRACING is a traditional design. It is the most common form of bracing, and is used in most Japanese guitars. The diagram shows five fan braces, though some models have as many as eleven.

(2) THE CROSS BRACE is used extensively on Country & Western (plectrum) guitars. It reinforces the face and also helps to promote a more full-bodied sound. Because the steel-strung guitar exerts a pressure on the bridge of five times that of its nylon-strung counterpart, the face could tend to lift if traditional forms of bracing were applied.

(1) FAN BRACING   (2) CROSS BRACE   (3) BOUCHET BAR BRACING   (4) TRANSVERSE BAR BRACING

(3) THE BOUCHET BAR is similar to the concept of violin construction in that sound posts are adjacent to the guitar bridge. The sound is 'sucked' along narrow suspended rods which join the face near the sound-hole. Sound is caught in the body and then 'locked' into the parts before being bounced along the grain and through the sound-hole.

(4) TRANSVERSE BAR bracing is designed along the lines of traditional fan strutting, but is barred so that either a greater treble or bass response may be obtained. The diagonal bar cut can be interchanged as required. The distance of the sound bounce between the final transverse bar and the sound-hole area will determine the type of control that can be exerted by the guitar itself.

The BACK resembles the face of the guitar but has fewer and less positive supports, thus allowing for a measured sound balance.

The SIDES enclose the instrument. Through their depth they also govern its sound production quality.

The neck: Extreme precision is needed in the crafting of this component, for the slightest miscalculation in the distances between the frets can adversely affect what might otherwise have been a good instrument.

The neck can be constructed from up to six separate cuts of wood, which in turn must be responsively harmonically balanced against the guitar body. Flaws of any kind are not acceptable.

The head can be a rather delicate unit. It is joined to the neck and, if badly constructed, can reduce the vibration responses of the neck against the body.

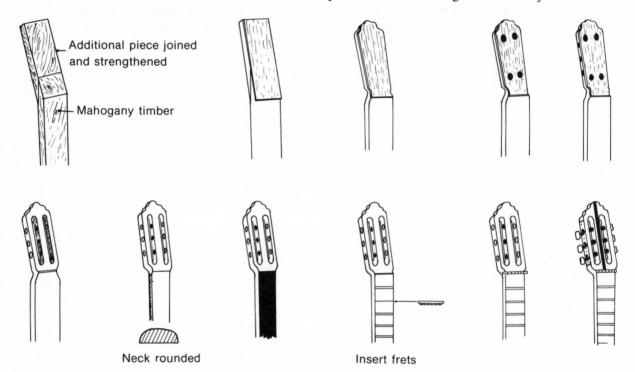

Additional piece joined and strengthened

Mahogany timber

Neck rounded   Insert frets

How a guitar is crafted

The steps briefly outlined in this section apply in principle to the construction of all types of acoustic and acoustic electric guitars. The selection of the right materials is vital, and most woods used in making folk guitars are cured for four or more years under meticulous supervision. The emphasis at every stage of manufacture is on craft and, in most cases, on the patient creation by hand of all major parts.

Guitar necks, for instance, are carved by hand from carefully selected straight-grained hardwoods and are then fitted to sound boards of uniform thickness and ideal resonance *(Fig. 1)*.

A special jig is used to form permanent body contours. The cut sheets of wood are first made pliable by bathing in boiling (or almost boiling) water, and are then placed in the jig and allowed to stand under extreme heat. As the jig temperature drops the wooden sheets set in the shape dictated by the jig, a process known as thermo-shaping *(Fig. 2)*.

The thermo-shaped side boards of the body are held in place on the combined neck and face unit by strong, thin wedges before being securely glued and then chisel-trimmed. Additional bracing is added, and preparations are made for fitting the back board (the neck unit is sometimes added after the body assembly has been completed), *(Fig. 3)*.

When the back, sides and sound board have been joined, the edges are trimmed with strips of white celluloid and mosaic woodwork to protect the sides (edges) and to further enhance the graceful edges of the body. Equal care is applied to the fitting of the marquetry or inlays in the patterns outlining the sound-hole *(Fig. 4)*.

Fig. 1

Fig. 4

Fig. 2

Fig. 5

Fig. 3

Fig. 6

Ebony, one of the hardest and most handsome of woods, is used for the fingerboard and the bridge. Frets of nickel silver are set deeply and at correct spacings to ensure faultless pitch. Finally, the deep and lustrous finish of the sound boards is produced by the application of several coats of lacquer followed by thorough hand-buffing *(Fig. 5)*.

This photograph shows completed body shapes drying out slowly in controlled temperature and humidity conditions prior to finishing and lacquering *(Fig. 6)*.

CHAPTER 3

Choosing Your Guitar

Buying your first guitar

If you are an absolute beginner, buying your first instrument will probably produce a mixture of excitement and confusion. You will be elated at satisfying the dream of being able to make your own music, but baffled by the seemingly infinite range of types, varieties and prices.

To avoid disappointment, seek the advice of an expert. If you are planning to learn with a teacher, let him be your guide. You will also receive good advice from most retail stores that also have teaching studios because they must be prepared to back the quality of the instruments they sell in order to maintain the reputation of their teaching standards.

The best instrument for a beginner is one fitted with nylon strings. The sound of this type of guitar is far more mellow than that of its steel-strung counterpart, and the nylon-strung guitar usually has only about one fifth of the string pressure of steel-strung models in the lower price range. Another benefit is the wider fingerboard, which will facilitate clearer production and thus make your progress easier and faster.

The right price to pay, without spending too much, is one of the main problems you will meet. Naturally, the more you pay the better will be the quality. On the other hand, a poorly constructed instrument (being cheaper) may seem a very attractive proposition because of its bargain price. You might think that the cheaper model will do as a 'trial' instrument while you're learning, or until you can afford to buy a better guitar—but you must appreciate that your 'bargain' might prove impossible to learn on; this, inevitably, would impair your progress and you might even decide never to play (or try to play) again after your first fruitless lessons.

You should be able to buy a reasonable guitar for approximately half of the average national weekly wage. This price should in fact buy you an instrument that will mature or improve with age (even with normal abuse) and that could give good musical and sound production for a minimum of ten years.

Not every type of guitar on the market is suitable for someone who is about to start learning to play. You should therefore be aware not only of the different types but also of the basic differences between the various types.

A review of some of the different types available:

(1) The Classical Guitar

The finger-style, classical or folk guitar is completely traditional in style, and is distinguished from all other types in having nylon or gut strings. It has a flat top with a round 'mosaic' hole. The neck is six to seven centimetres wide, and the instrument is usually played with a plucking or stroking motion.

The strings on this style of guitar are set wide apart, and the fingerboard of the concert model may be up to eight centimetres wide. Its low-pressure strings, rich tone and ease of fingering make it an ideal instrument for the beginner.

(2) The Plectrum Guitar

Throughout the world today the most commonly used member of the guitar family is the plectrum (steel-strung) guitar. Models in the plectrum range include:

Country & Western guitar
12-string jumbo guitar
Jazz F-hole guitar
Electric F-hole cutaway guitar
Semi-acoustic electric guitar
Acoustic electric flat top guitar
Electric 12-string guitar
Solid body electric guitar

These instruments come in a variety of shapes and sizes, but they all function in the same manner and are tuned in the same way (Spanish). Although styles of expression and interpretation may change with each performer, the method of muscular technique (control) remains constant throughout the plectrum guitar range. Thus, having mastered the basic guitar-playing techniques you can interchange models as you wish.

The Country & Western guitar (flat top): This has a much larger body and a narrower neck than the finger-style or classical guitar; in fact, the Country & Western guitar is often referred to as a jumbo or flat top model. The body also tends to be much heavier in construction since standard gauge steel strings usually generate an additional 100 pounds of pressure on the bridge.

However, its characteristics are much the same as those of the classical guitar. The overall sound of the instrument tends to be sharp yet full-bodied in tone.

The 12-string guitar: This model is the 'big brother' of the jumbo or C&W guitar. Although similar in most respects it has an even larger body and a far wider neck to accommodate the extra six strings (making twelve strings in all). The twelve strings are tuned:

1 – 2 – 3 – 4   in unison pairs
5 – 6 – 7 – 8   in one-octave pairs
9 – 10 – 11 – 12   in two-octave pairs

Each pair of strings is in turn tuned to the traditional Spanish tuning.

The F-hole guitar: This is similar to the C&W guitar, but has a 'shaped face' instead of the usual flat top and F-holes instead of the round sound-hole. The F-holes, like those of a violin, are cut at the extreme widths of the face to provide even distribution of sound.

In many aspects of construction, apart from the body cutaway, it duplicates the violin body, and it is not uncommon to find models with sound posts (replacing braces) as required in violin construction.

Electric acoustic F-hole guitar: An amplified version of the standard F-hole guitar.

Acoustic electric (flat top) jumbo guitar: An amplified version of the Country & Western guitar.

Semi-acoustic electric guitar: A slim-bodied F-hole guitar that relies heavily on magnetic impulses through an amplifier to produce sound. Because of the soft volume return from the body shape the essential points to look for in this guitar are a well-manufactured neck and good pick-ups.

Solid body electric guitar: Unlike other plectrum guitars, the solid body guitar relies entirely on amplification to produce sound. The solid wooden body combats the feedback problem common to most other electric guitars since the solid wood does not resonate beyond a very short distance with any great volume.

The solid body does not, of course, require a hollow 'sound box', and the body shape does not therefore have to follow the traditional guitar design. Many models in this style are quite radically 'contemporary' in shape.

Classical guitar   Country & Western guitar   12-string guitar   Electric acoustic F-hole guitar

Pickup

Tone control

Aluminum bone saddle   Volume control

Acoustic electric
(flat top) jumbo guitar   Semi-acoustic electric guitar   Solid body electric guitar

Features of the flat top acoustic electric guitar

Of all the plectrum (steel-strung) guitars that the novice might decide to buy, this is the most versatile. Unlike the classical or finger-style guitar, it has steel instead of gut or nylon strings and must therefore be played with a plectrum; and, unlike its non-electric brother, the Country & Western guitar, it can be plugged into an amplifier. It is, all in all, a good instrument on which to learn, particularly if you wish to progress to semi-acoustic or solid body guitars.

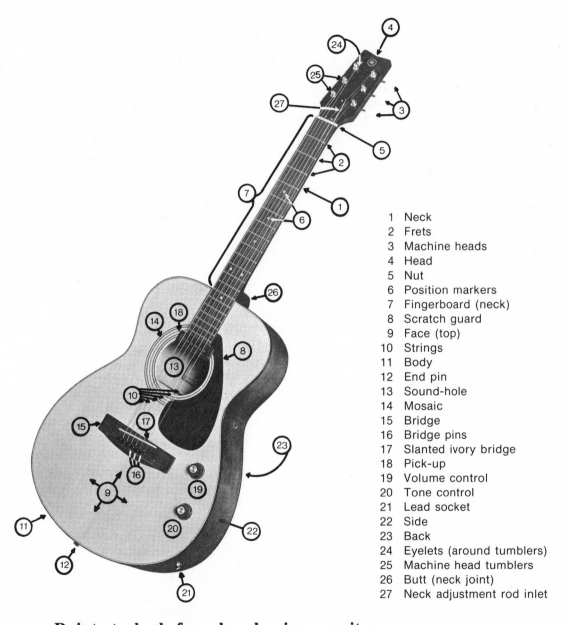

1 Neck
2 Frets
3 Machine heads
4 Head
5 Nut
6 Position markers
7 Fingerboard (neck)
8 Scratch guard
9 Face (top)
10 Strings
11 Body
12 End pin
13 Sound-hole
14 Mosaic
15 Bridge
16 Bridge pins
17 Slanted ivory bridge
18 Pick-up
19 Volume control
20 Tone control
21 Lead socket
22 Side
23 Back
24 Eyelets (around tumblers)
25 Machine head tumblers
26 Butt (neck joint)
27 Neck adjustment rod inlet

Points to look for when buying a guitar

The following points will be helpful if you want to buy a quality instrument but have doubts about the advice being given or the ability of the salesman to recommend a good instrument for the price you can afford.

Check body for cracks or loose braces: Hold the guitar upright and slowly (but firmly) tap the back of the body with your middle finger. If you hear anything but a 'banjo-type' resonance, check again. Rattles usually mean trouble with a capital T, the cause being either a crack in the body or a loose or broken brace support.

Check neck for warping: Hold the neck of the guitar, with the body of the instrument away from you, and sight along it for any edge irregularities on either side of the neck. Some guitars have a curved (convex) neck, and this should not be confused with warping.

Check neck thickness: If the neck appears to be as deep as it is wide, return it to the shelf immediately. A reasonable depth is usually half that of the width.

Check smoothness of frets: Check for loose or protruding frets by running your fingers along both edges of the neck. If the instrument does not feel comfortable or smooth, compare it with the feel of a different and preferably more expensive model. Badly protruding frets will hamper control and may cut or abrase your fingers.

Check string height: Normally the strings should lie no more than 5 mm above the twelfth fret or 2 mm above the first fret. An instrument with higher strings will restrict your control of playing speed.

Check clarity of notes: Each note should be 'stopped' on each fret over the total length of the neck. You should do this for at least one string, and preferably more, making sure that the string does not rattle or buzz. A badly constructed fingerboard will inhibit your progress.

Caring for your guitar

Far too many people take an instrument for granted. Abuse is not uncommon and unfortunately tends to shorten the life-span of a guitar.

Ignorance contributes most to constant (if unintentional) abuse. Many abuses, such as rough handling and dropping, can be appreciated easily enough, but many important abuses are overlooked or never considered. Always keep the following points in mind if you want to get maximum life and service from your guitar.

Storage: If possible, always store your guitar in a hard case or pack the outside of the instrument with crepe-cardboard to avoid accidental damage. If you intend storing it for a long time, loosen or remove the strings.

Although hanging a guitar on a wall might look decorative, don't do it—hanging puts unnatural strains on the instrument and can cause permanent damage.

Temperature and humidity: Extremes of temperature and humidity, and sudden changes in either or both, can warp or crack the guitar body and can damage or even destroy its natural tone. Imported guitars are particularly vulnerable to this kind of damage since the glues used in their manufacture may not stand up to your local climatic conditions.

Always try to keep your guitar in a draught-free room with a constant temperature (or at least with minimum temperature and humidity fluctuations). *Never* leave it inside a car with the windows up, or in the boot of a car—especially in hot weather or full sunlight.

Cracks: If cracks appear, consult a qualified repairer *immediately*. *Never* attempt to repair cracks yourself. If your instrument cracks in the course of normal use within three months of purchase, see your dealer—your instrument should still be under warranty. Even if cracks are the result of abuse, the damage may not be irreparable—but have them seen to quickly, for the longer they remain without treatment the worse the damage will become.

Loose fixed bridge: This is generally caused by over-tension (tuning too high, too often) and should only be repaired by an expert. Incorrect realignment of the fixed bridge, to even the slightest degree, could put the instrument out of tune for ever. Don't tackle this seemingly easy repair job yourself.

Loose strut or brace: Any rattle inside the body should be inspected immediately by an expert. If one of the internal body braces has worked loose it will weaken the structure of the guitar—and a problem of this nature will not correct itself.

PART TWO
Introducing the six strings

CHAPTER 4

Preparation

The strings of the guitar

The strings are named in order from the first to the sixth (from the thinnest to the thickest):

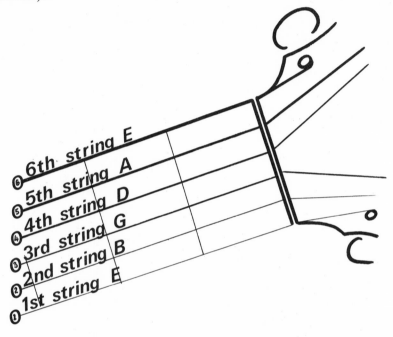

The names can be memorised easily with the help of this sentence:

EASTER BUNNIES GET DRUNK AT EASTER

Easter	first string	E	(thinnest)
Bunnies	second string	B	
Get	third string	G	
Drunk	fourth string	D	
At	fifth string	A	
Easter	sixth string	E	(thickest)

Although this aid can be used with great success you must, as soon as possible, be able to name the strings in order without having to refer to the sentence.

How to change nylon strings: Strings should be replaced one at a time (starting with the sixth) so as not to change the tension of the guitar suddenly.

Insert each string through the appropriate hole in the bridge and wind the short end two or three times around the longer end. This 'knot' will hold securely under tension.

The further end of the string is inserted in the appropriate hole in the machine head and wound around itself once or twice before tensioning.

Do not over-tune the strings (see methods of tuning on pages 24, 30, 67, 90, 106), and do not put steel strings on a nylon-strung guitar.

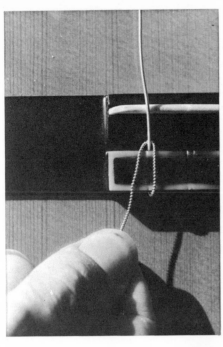
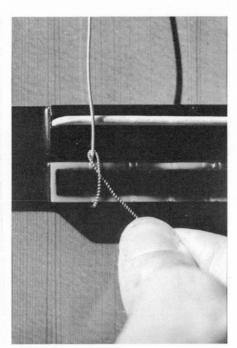

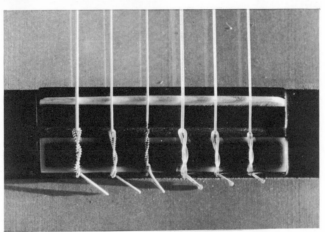

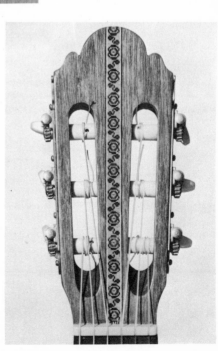

How to change steel strings: Pull the string through the bridge, bridge-plate or bridge pin hole, taking care not to knot the string in the process.

Wind the further end through the protruding machine head, allowing at least three turns before applying tension.

Do not put steel strings on a nylon-strung (finger-style or classical) guitar—steel strings exert five times the bridge pressure of nylon strings.

Tuning the guitar

Pitch-pipe tuning: Although there are many different methods of tuning a guitar, as a beginner you will achieve the best results (at this elementary stage) by using a pitch-pipe.

Each of the six pitch-pipe reeds resonates at the approximate sound of the corresponding string of the guitar. You need only duplicate (to the best of your ability) each pitch against each of the strings to obtain reasonable tuning.

As your music hearing improves the experience gained from pitch-pipe tuning will allow you to graduate to more advanced forms of tuning and to achieve far more accurate results.

Unison tuning: To apply unison tuning you need only be able to recognise identical pitch from another string.

Using a tuning fork (or any other constant pitch), tune the first string (E). The second string is tuned to the first by placing a finger behind the fifth fret (fifth metal bar) and turning the machine head (cog) until the pitch is identical to that of the open first string.

To tune the remaining strings: press behind the fourth fret of the third string (G) and tune to the open second string; press behind the fifth fret of the fourth string (D) and tune to the open third string; press behind the fifth fret of the fifth string (A) and tune to the open fourth string; press behind the fifth fret of the sixth string (E) and tune to the open fifth string.

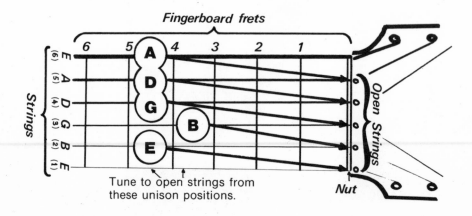

Tune to open strings from these unison positions.

The reverse method (starting at the sixth string) can also be used, but this is far harder to manipulate and it is more difficult to obtain the exacting result required.

The higher the pitch the easier it is to recognise on a fretted instrument. It is thus much easier to recognise the exact sound of the first string than that of the sixth string—and therefore to be far more accurate in tuning.

Irrespective of the method used, the guitar cannot be tuned successfully with worn strings. Strings should be changed at least once a month to maintain harmonic balance. Constant string replacement allows the ear to develop quickly and to recognise the same sound continually, thus promoting a sharper awareness of exact pitch.

Fingers of the left hand

The fingers of the left hand are numbered from one to four (from the index finger to the small finger). The thumb is not generally used for playing, but helps support the wrist correctly in its relationship to the guitar.

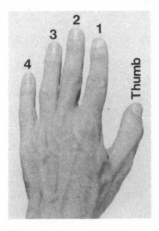

Holding the guitar

The guitar must at all times be held in a relaxed position. You should not recline back in a chair; nor should you hold the instrument to suit your usual sitting manner—you must sit to suit the guitar.

To achieve a good sitting position use a backless chair, or sit as far forward as practicable towards the edge of an upright chair. Do not slouch or lean backwards while playing—and *never* practise on a bed or lounge chair.

The greatest muscular control can be obtained by crossing your right leg over your left leg. Place the guitar waist over the right leg, with the face in a vertical line from the floor, at the same time holding the instrument

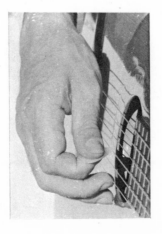

comfortably against your body. Put your right arm over the body of the guitar, allowing sufficient room to move your wrist comfortably while also adding support to the instrument.

The left-hand wrist *must not support the guitar*. Its main purpose is to add support to the individual fingers, allowing comfortable movement in a spider-like manner over the fingerboard.

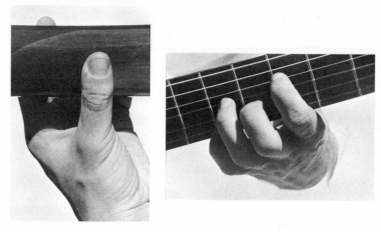

Always hold your left thumb directly and firmly behind the neck at a spot centrally located between the span of the left-hand fingers in use. If your thumb overlaps the neck it will restrict the potential of your left hand for accuracy and speed.

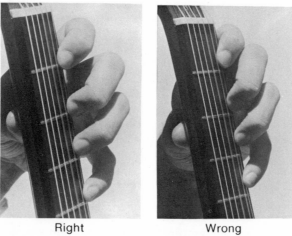

Right   Wrong

Always play the left-hand fingers in a straight and cupped manner. If you let them fall sideways they may cause 'buzzing' and restrict the sound of the desired note(s).

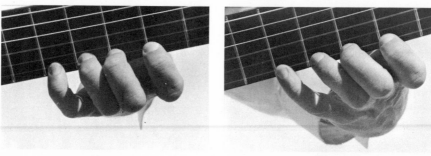

Right   Wrong

All left-hand fingernails should be cut to, or below, the level of the fingertips. Long nails will greatly interfere with the correct use of the left-hand fingers and wrist.

Wrong: nails too long

Basic elements of musical theory

Names of the notes: Music is written diagrammatically with the aid of notes. The notes are named after the first seven letters of the alphabet:

A B C D E F G

At the completion of note 'G' the pattern begins again at note 'A', maintaining the same order:

A B C D E F G   A B C D E F G   A B C etc.

It is important to realise that although notes may share identical names they may be placed in a variety of positions within the written musical compass. By investigating the two (or more) notes that share the same name it will be seen (or, more accurately, heard) that their individual pitch will differ, with one note being higher in sound than another note sharing the same name, and vice versa.

The G or treble clef is the only signature used for the reading of music on the guitar, and is placed at the beginning of each line of music.

The staff or stave: The five lines and four spaces upon which music is written are called the staff or stave.

Notes falling on any of the lines, or the spaces between, are given specific names (pitches). The individual lines and spaces are also numbered for reference and ease of learning.

Notes on the lines:

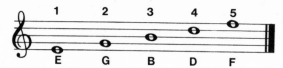

These can be easily memorised by taking each given note (letter) and forming the sentence:

EVERY GOOD BOY DOES FINE

Notes in the spaces:

The spaces can be memorised by forming the individual notes into the word:

F A C E

The notation of music: Verbal notation has been written in two separate forms throughout this book. Both forms are used (almost always separately) in the many books, tutors and methods available today; the simultaneous use of both forms will help you to avoid confusion as and when you refer to music in other books.

The first of these forms uses the English Method, derived from Latin terms that are very similar to modern Italian terms, and is generally shown here in small capitals:

CROTCHET, MINIM, etc.

The second uses the American Method, devised early in this century, and is shown in brackets immediately after its English equivalent:

(Quarter Note), (Half Note), etc.

THE MOST COMMON NOTES IN USE TODAY

𝅝 SEMI-BREVE	(Whole Note)	4 beats	
𝅗𝅥 MINIM	(Half Note)	2 beats	(one half of the value of the SEMI-BREVE note)
𝅘𝅥 CROTCHET	(Quarter Note)	1 beat	(one quarter of the value of the SEMI-BREVE note or one half the value of the MINIM note)
𝅘𝅥𝅮 QUAVER	(Eighth Note)	½ beat	(one eighth of the value of the SEMI-BREVE note)
𝅘𝅥𝅯 SEMI-QUAVER	(Sixteenth Note)	¼ beat	(one sixteenth of the value of the SEMI-BREVE note)

The formation of these notes can be easily memorised by taking the note of the largest value and progressively halving the value of each successive note.

The note of largest value in use today is the SEMI-BREVE (Whole Note). By adding a stem to this note its value is halved, and it is now called a MINIM (Half Note). The system can be applied to any of these five notes simply by adding the appropriate stems or flags.

CHAPTER 5

Basic Rhythm

Rhythm

A natural phenomenon, such as one's heartbeat, is man's first subconscious experience of rhythm. In fact, man seems unable to exist without demanding conscious rhythms such as groupings of accents (music) or cadences in poetry and speech (theatre)—or such rhythmic actions as a constant tapping of fingers while attempting to relax, when rhythm is a means of satisfying some minor forms of neurosis.

If we open our eyes, as well as our ears, we can find rhythm all around us in many shapes and forms.

For example, natural rhythm can be the constant movement of leaves on a tree as the wind passes through them, or the motion of waves on a beach. Mechanical rhythm can be the purr of a car's engine, or the quiet ticking of a watch. And physical rhythm, although rarely thought of, can be the regular action of breathing or the continual blinking of the eyelids.

Whatever the type of rhythm, and whatever its cause, some basic need compels man to promote rhythm through his music. The listener will also experience the sensation of rhythm through inward motion, although at times this may be experienced in a manner that can be likened to mechanical calculation. Nevertheless, rhythm is present and, what is more important, is present constantly.

Carl Seashore, in *Psychology of Music* (1938), defined rhythm as 'an instinctive disposition to group recurrent sense impressions vividly and with precision, mainly by time or intensity or both, in such a way as to derive pleasure and efficiency through the groupings'.

Devoting time and effort to the analysis and understanding of rhythm is a pleasurable pursuit. It is also a practical means of furthering your comprehension of music.

Time signatures

The time signature is one of the most important factors in music. It not only permits the construction of music to a given pattern but also governs the rhythm to be used and, to a great extent, also provides the basis of musical expression.

Although the individual style of playing can alter, the performer cannot avoid understanding the meaning of the time signature in its written context.

In written form the time signature is a grouping of separate numerals, one placed on top of the other in the style of a mathematical fraction. However, a line must not be placed between the two numerals:

$$\frac{4}{4} \text{ or } \frac{3}{2} \text{ or } \frac{6}{8} \quad but\ not \quad \frac{4}{4} \text{ or } \frac{3}{2} \text{ or } \frac{6}{8}$$

The function of the time signature is to tell the performer, at a glance, how the music is to be counted and played. Whenever a time signature is being read it must be dissected into two separate areas, the upper and the lower:

THE UPPER SECTION
(The Top Line)

The top line represents the *number of beats* to be used. Therefore, if the upper section supports the numeral 4, it is simply expressed as 'four'. The most common numerals found in the top line are:

2 – 3 – 4 – 6 – 8 – 9 – 12

THE LOWER SECTION
(The Bottom Line)

The bottom line denotes the *type of beat* to be used. Each numeral is directly associated with a specified note value which, when coupled with the top line numerals, provides the time signature formula.

4   means   CROTCHET (Quarter Note) bar value
2   means   MINIM (Half Note) bar value
8   means   QUAVER (Eighth Note) bar value
16   means   SEMI-QUAVER (Sixteenth Note) bar value

Therefore the time signature is to be read in the following manner:

4   (number of beats)   four
4   (type of beat)   CROCHET (Quarter Note)

In other words, 4 means:

Four CROTCHET *beats to a bar*
or
Four Quarter Note *beats to a bar*

Bars and measures

A bar is a measure of time between two vertical lines placed on the staff (stave) and related to the time signature.

The measure (bar) is always flanked by a bar line and its value is always governed by the time signature, which stabilises its total time value.

The bar line is a vertical line separating one measure of time from another.

A double bar line ends a given passage (piece or part) of music. Although the use of a double bar line is more commonly applied at the end of a passage of music, it can also apply during the melody.

Within a melody there are usually an introduction, a chorus and an ending. The sectional double bar line can be used to indicate any of these sections, even though they are still part of the same song. The final double bar line is always used at the end of any piece of music.

Pitch-pipe tuning

Select the strings that need tuning by comparing, in turn, the pitch of each string with the sound of the equivalent note on the pitch-pipe. If a string is out of tune, turn the appropriate machine head while blowing on the reed until the string and reed notes are identical.

It is recommended that when you have completed tuning with the pitch-pipe, check the tuning by the unison method (page 24).

Pitch-pipes tend to lose their notes (pitch) rather quickly since the metallic reeds are prone to rust. To ensure a longer life for the pitch-pipe, tap it immediately after use; it is also advisable to suck hard on the reeds from time to time.

Using the plectrum

The many different schools of thought on the use of a plectrum advocate many different styles of application. The application most often recommended, and the one recommended here, is the use of the plectrum as *an extension of the right-hand thumb tip*, for brushing the thumb tip lightly over the strings tends to be the most natural way to play the guitar.

Never let any more than a quarter of an inch (5 to 8 mm) of plectrum protrude beyond the tip of the thumb. The more plectrum that protrudes, the less natural the feel, and consequently the greater the chance of mistakes.

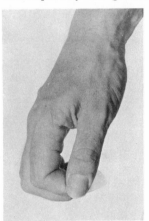

Correct plectrum grip, with limited protrusion and relaxed wrist.

Always apply the plectrum with a downward motion (down-stroke). Do not use the up-stroke until recommended in this tutor.

Use of the plectrum allows for natural muscular movements of the wrist, and the way in which the plectrum is held must not interfere with these natural movements. If the thumb tip is used for playing without the use of the plectrum, the position naturally assumed by the wrist will restrict the correct use of the fingers should you later wish to apply the finger-style technique of guitar playing.

Never use a 'thumb-pick'. This tends to dislodge the hand from its natural position and it generally restricts movement, for up-strokes are extremely difficult to play correctly with a thumb-pick.

Some useful hints

Timing in music: You should be totally aware of timing in music. Such knowledge will facilitate control and the application of independent notation, and will help you to avoid guesswork.

Remember that each note not only resembles a pitch, but also commands a certain duration of vibration.

The counting of time in music: Always count the bar value aloud after determining the counting shown by the time signature. The duration between beats must be absolutely even.

Always play slowly, so as not to break the continuing rhythmic sequence of each beat, until you have acquired a firm knowledge of the guitar fingerboard.

To maintain a continually smooth sound, count each beat of the bar *aloud*. This will not only make you more aware of the importance of timing, but will also direct you to the following note in its bar position and will help you to avoid mistakes while playing the selected passage. If at any time you find that you are groping, or continually allowing mistakes to develop, *slow down*.

Your first playing of a passage should be performed by *sight*. It should not differ from the final performance except that the final playing will be faster (due to increased confidence) as your awareness of each note's pitch and value is enhanced by the correct approach.

Know each note you play: You must be aware not only of each note in its written position but also of its pitch name. If you play each elementary passage twice—once by the name of the note, and the second time by the time signature beat—your progress will be greatly enhanced.

Whenever you meet a note beyond one beat in duration, name it accordingly but play it only as written. By simulating the beats (from the name of each note in its time value) the two systems will both result in the same final performance. The two-beat note is simply named twice (E, E rather than one, two) and is still played *only* on the first of the two beats.

CHAPTER 6

Elementary Theory, Notation and Diagrammatical Chord Accompaniments

Notes on the First String

The neck fingerboard diagram: The use of this diagram (left, above) is a popular means of learning to play the guitar without having to read music. The grid represents the relationship of strings to frets on the fingerboard:

vertical lines	=	strings
horizontal lines	=	frets
circled numerals	=	fingers of the left hand
small circles	=	'open string' sound

How to count the crotchet (quarter note) beat

The CROTCHET (Quarter Note) is valued at one beat. One CROTCHET (Quarter Note) note should be played each time your foot strikes the ground.

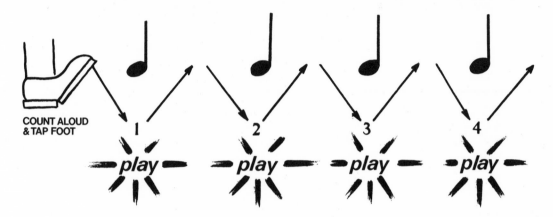

Exercise on the First String
(incorporating crotchets)

How to use the time signature: The time signature denotes the actual measure of time found within the compass of a bar. 4 means *four* CROTCHET *beats to a bar*.
4

Each CROTCHET (Quarter Note) note is one beat in length, therefore the time signature gives each bar a total value of four beats.

How to count the minim (half note) beat

The MINIM (Half Note) is valued at two beats. The note is played on the first of the foot taps and held for the next successive beat only.

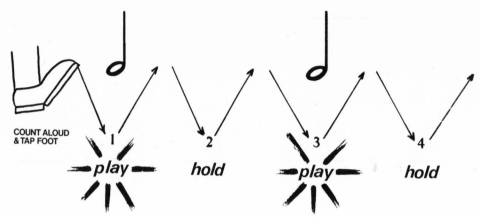

Exercise on the First String
(incorporating minims)

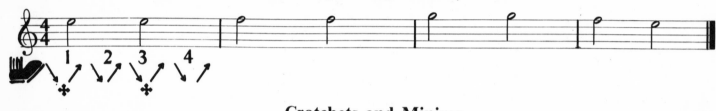

Crotchets and Minims

Exercise on the First String No. 1

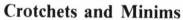

Exercise on the First String No. 2

How to count a semi-breve (whole note) beat

The SEMI-BREVE (Whole Note) is valued at four beats. The note is played on the beat of one and held for the next three successive beats.

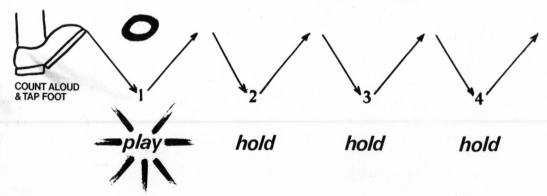

Exercise on the First String
(incorporating semi-breves)

Exercise on the First String No. 3

Exercise on the First String No. 4

Exercise on the First String No. 5

Exercise on the First String No. 6

Exercise on the First String No. 7

Exercise on the First String No. 8

Exercise on the First String No. 9

Reminder: The left hand must not be used to support the guitar. The only part of the left hand to be applied to the guitar is the thumb joint (for an open string); do not put your fingers along the edge of the neck or fingerboard to support your left hand.

Notes on the Second String

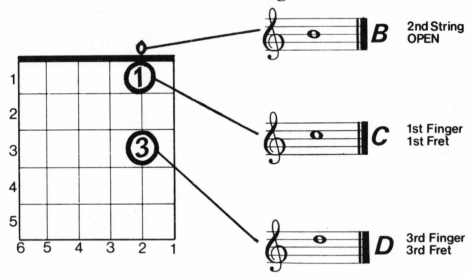

B   **2nd String OPEN**

C   **1st Finger 1st Fret**

D   **3rd Finger 3rd Fret**

Exercise on the Second String No. 1

Exercise on the Second String No. 2

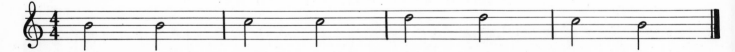

Exercise on the Second String No. 3

Exercise on the Second String No. 4

Common time: The time signature **C** replaces the value $\frac{4}{4}$ and is known as common time.

Exercise on the Second String No. 5

Fingering: In order to develop and maintain a correct technique, apply the following approach *unless otherwise stated:*

first finger	–	first fret
second finger	–	second fret
third finger	–	third fret
fourth finger	–	fourth fret
fourth finger	–	fifth fret

If at any stage you cannot extend your finger to the required fret (e.g., fourth finger to fifth fret), move your whole wrist higher along the neck so that you can obtain the desired note comfortably without awkward stretching. This will ensure that the correct technique is employed at all times. *Do not turn your wrist (or hand) to obtain that extended note.*

Spring Breeze

Paper Dolls

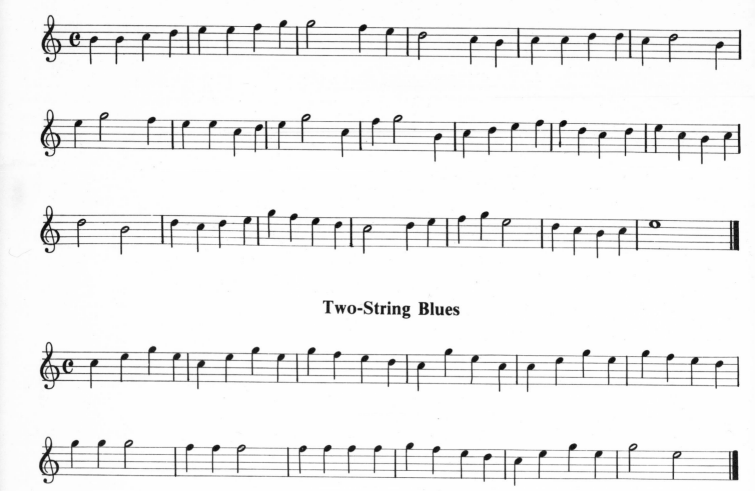

Two-String Blues

Going Places

The guitar chord diagram

A chord is any combination of a succession of notes played simultaneously. The guitar chord diagram is an extension of the neck fingerboard diagram.

The diagram was originally devised as an aid to guitarists in some of the more difficult chord and finger progressions. Its use at this stage of your development is designed to give you the opportunity, through daily practice, of developing the muscles and control of your left-hand fingers. It is not intended to teach you how to *play* chords at this point, but rather to *prepare* your left-hand fingering so that you will not be unduly frustrated by a lack of fingering ability when you first meet chords in their full musical context.

In its basic 'grid' form the guitar chord diagram duplicates the neck fingerboard of the guitar;

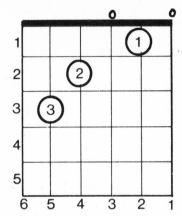

Vertical lines = strings: These parallel lines represent the six strings, and are numbered 1 to 6 reading from right to left.

Horizontal lines = frets: These parallel lines represent the frets, the narrow metal bars that protrude above the surface of the fingerboard. When you apply your fingers to the specified strings, your fingertips must fall as close as possible to the edges of the frets; in this way you will attain maximum control with minimum effort.

Circled numerals = fingers of the left hand: Each finger of the left hand is numbered 1 to 4 from the index finger to the small finger. The thumb is rarely used, and is not numbered.

Small circles above grid = 'open string' sound: An open string is one that is sounded without any of the left-hand fingers being applied to it.

Total number of strings to be played: The only strings to be strummed are those with circled numbers on them and those with circles above them (open strings). *No other string is to be played.*

Always strum from the thickest to the thinnest string: Always play or strum the strings with a downward motion (down-stroke) to produce an effect similar to the 'roll of a harp'. With a direct and firm right-hand sweep carry the plectrum across the total number of strings specified in the guitar chord diagram:

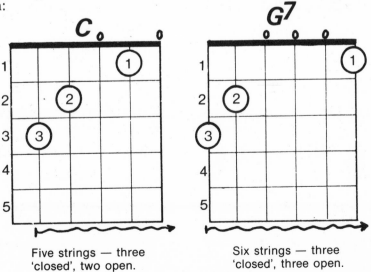

Five strings — three 'closed', two open.

Six strings — three 'closed', three open.

Playing chords

The playing of chords must be approached with the same careful attention to timing that is demanded by individual notes.

Because a chord is more difficult to manipulate (finger) than any single note on its own, practise at first at a speed that allows you to change without difficulty to the next chord—if this takes ten seconds at present, play each beat at ten-second intervals. If you follow this method it will take only a short time before you become accustomed to changing faster until you reach the desired speed. *Abuse this principle*, and you may never play or change chords correctly.

Applying chords to music: Within the framework of musical notation chords can be shown in a number of different ways. Where guitar chords are used as an accompaniment they are commonly written in this form:

Alternatively, the chord accompaniment can be written below a stave on which a melodic line has been notated, and two performers can thus read and play from the same passage of music—one playing the melody, the other accompanying with chords.

Each beat is shown as a stroke or chord symbol. Do not change chords until the following one is shown, and then continue that chord until the next chord change, and so on.

Dotted notes

A dot placed on the right-hand side of a note prolongs the value of that note by half of its original given value:

MINIM (Half Note)	$\textstyle\downarrow$	2 beats
DOTTED MINIM (Dotted Half Note)	$\textstyle\downarrow$.	3 beats (2 beats plus a half of 2 beats = 1)

Snowflakes

40

Beautiful Brown Eyes

Ability to play in time with another: Your approach to timing will be incorrect *until* you are able to play in time with another guitarist. You should therefore play and practise with someone else as soon as you can (if this is practicable). Not only will both of you achieve greater control of timing, but you will also develop a greater feeling for the melody being attempted. If you have no-one to practise with, playing duets by yourself with the aid of a tape-recorder is an invaluable aid in helping to overcome incorrect timing (see page 43).

The following piece is a perfect example of a simple duet. Practise both the melody line and the chords and, if you are playing with someone else, alternate between melody and chords so that you learn to control the timing of both.

Long Long Ago

Suffering from sore fingers? If you have come this far with plenty of practice your fingertips will be reasonably sore. There is very little you can do to combat this problem, although one solution is to shorten your practice times. You may wish to rub methylated spirits or methyl alcohol onto your fingertips prior to playing, for this will act as a temporary anaesthetic until callouses develop. Buttering the fingertips, and similar 'cures', can be dismissed as old wives' tales and should be avoided. They bring little or no relief, and only tend to keep the fingertips soft.

Additional Note on the First String

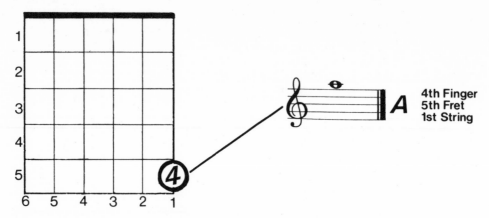

4th Finger
5th Fret
1st String

Do not stretch to the fifth fret: It is of the utmost importance that you do not try to stretch to the fifth fret from the hand position specified for the first three (or four) frets. Instead, slide your wrist upwards along the neck so that you can play the note A comfortably without twisting your wrist out of its correct position.

You would obviously find it impractical to stretch to the tenth fret, so why attempt to stretch to the fifth!

London Bridge

Approach all music *slowly* at first so that you begin to learn to *sight-read each passage of music*. As you become better acquainted with the fingerboard notation your speed will increase naturally, and you will avoid repetition and consistent mistakes.

Abide with Me

Prepare each chord mentally before you play it: Sight-reading ahead, as many beats in advance as possible, will enable you to prepare mentally for each chord well before it has to be played. This will help you maintain the structure of the passage. You will be mentally prepared in terms of what fingers to use and where, and by the time you reach the chord in the music the playing of it should only be a matter of the correct finger placement.

The farther ahead you prepare the chord the easier it will be to quicken the tempo of the chord accompaniment; this will enhance even execution and eliminate time loss between chord changes.

The stem of a note

The stem of a note, as found in a MINIM (Half Note), CROTCHET (Quarter Note) or QUAVER (Eighth Note), can be written in an upward or downward position depending on where it is used within the staff.

Notes above the third line of the staff must have their stems written downwards:

Notes below the third line of the staff must have their stems written upwards:

Any note falling on the third line of the staff can have its stem written either upwards or downwards, depending on the notes around it within the bar. If other notes within the bar are written downwards, the notes on the third line must follow that style. If the bar is mixed (stems up and down) the stem of the note on the third line is then written to balance out the bar concerned, allowing for as much equalisation of stemming as possible.

If there is any doubt as to the position the stem on the third line must take, place (write) it downwards:

It is also essential to realise that whatever the position of the stem it must pass through (or touch) the third line of the staff on which it is being written.

General hints on improving your playing

The use of a tape-recorder: By using a tape-recorder you will hear any timing deficiencies and lack of clarity of notes. This can be an invaluable aid, for at this elementary stage there is so much to concentrate on that you cannot in fact hear or properly appreciate as much as ninety per cent of what you are playing while you are playing it.

With the aid of a tape-recorder you will hear exactly what you play (as it is heard by others), and this should help you by-pass a great deal of corrective work (either on your own, which is difficult, or with the guidance of a teacher). By hearing your mistakes, and knowing exactly where the problems lie, the frustration of correcting errors will be reduced to a minimum.

One of the greatest advantages of using a tape-recorder is that you can use it to play duets with yourself by playing the relative chord to the previously recorded written music, and vice versa, each being pace-set by the other.

Do not stop for mistakes: Mistakes are generally made because your reading capacity is usually slower than the speed you are attempting; or, to put it another way, you are probably not playing slowly enough to realise that a mistake is about to occur. Practise the same passage more slowly, at a speed at which you can read easily, and mistakes should be minimal.

If you stop to correct a mistake, one or more beats will be lost in correcting it (a mistake in itself) and further playings might perpetuate the mistake. *Do not stop for a mistake*—by-pass it, and on the next playing remember the area in which the mistake was made and try to avoid repeating it. If the same mistakes continue to occur, *slow down even more*. As the mistake is corrected you can again begin to play the passage at a faster tempo.

Simplifying control of the right hand: If it is realised that a miscalculation of about a quarter of an inch (5 to 8 mm), which is the distance between strings, can mean playing the wrong string, it is obvious that some means of assistance is necessary to help the positional judgement of the right hand. Plectrum guitarists (unlike finger-style guitarists) can achieve this by supporting the right hand on the body of the guitar, either with all their remaining available fingers (2, 3 or 4) or with the knuckle of the small right-hand finger (4).

Unlike the left hand, which must not support the guitar, the right hand is an excellent means of further stabilising the body of the guitar while at the same time assisting control of the notation being played.

The use of a metronome: The metronome, if used, *should be used sparingly* and only to correct timing deficiencies within a given passage.

Constant use of a metronome can lead to total reliance on the beat being allocated and generally to personal development as a 'mechanical musician'—one who is not fully aware of timing unless a metronome is used as an aid. Reliance on a metronome will gradually sever your ability to express music properly, with your playing usually performed a little out of time (just off the beat).

The metronome can be a tremendous asset to the musician, but if its application is abused it can become a nightmare.

Notes on the Third String

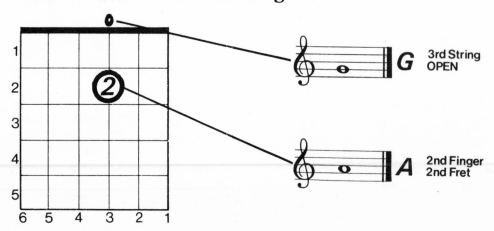

Learn to feel the fingerboard: You should, as quickly as possible, learn to play the notes by feeling the fret positions with your left hand; continual observation of the notational positions should be avoided. By applying this principle you will quickly learn to sight-read each note of music, will progress much faster, and will minimise the possibility of mistakes.

Exercise on the Third String No. 1

Exercise on the Third String No. 2

Exercise on the Third String No. 3

Round the Mulberry Bush

Jimmy Crack Corn

The octave

Whenever two notes have the same name, but are of different pitch (one written higher than the other, and vice versa), they are said to be an octave apart:

(OCTAVE APART)

An octave occurs when the pitch sequence is placed seven notes above (or below) the opening note:

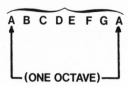

Each continuing sequence of seven successive notes will form a new octave:

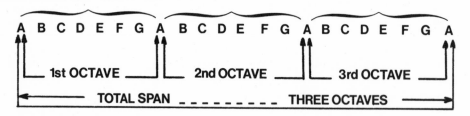

It is important to realise that an octave does not consist of eight notes, but is the eighth note above the first of a series of seven successive notes.

Repeat sign

The repeat sign is shown as a double bar line with dots above and below the third staff line. It simply means 'repeat the given passage':

You may repeat once only from the repeat sign inverted at the beginning of a passage:

If the inverted repeat sign is not used, repeat from the beginning of the melody:

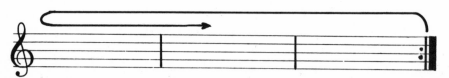

Three Four Time

Li'l 'Liza Jane

REPEAT FROM HERE

REPEAT AREA SHOWN

Tied notes

Whenever a curved line ⌣ is used to join together two notes of the same pitch, it is called a tie. The first note is played, and the value of the second note (which is *not* played) is added to that of the second note. The tied notes must be held for the total combined duration (value) of the two written notes.

Looby Loo

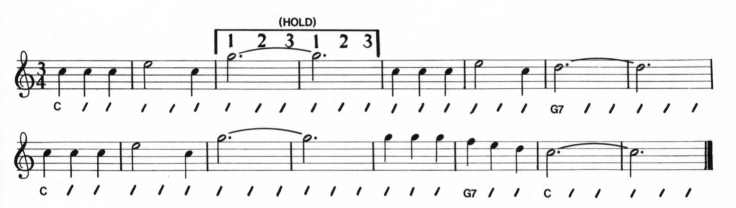

A tie adds to the allowable margin of a bar: Notes may now be extended (at the writer's pleasure) beyond the normal compass of a bar which, were it not for the tie, would be limited:

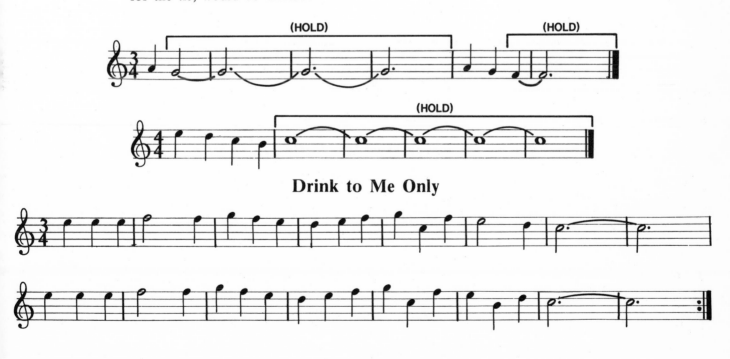

Drink to Me Only

Ten Little Indians

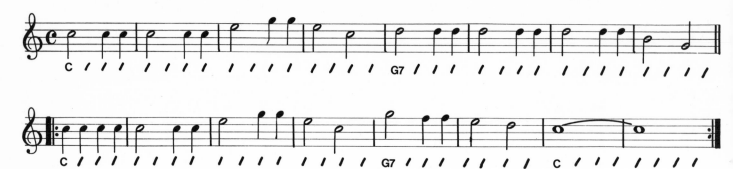

Bar repeats: Total bar repeat signs are often applied to music to avoid unnecessarily repetitive writing. In the case of orchestrated material, this repeat sign (𝄎) is often applied. The repeat sign has also proved invaluable in the repetitious tablature of the chord accompaniments found within music.

Music accompaniments are normally tabled like this:

Orchestrated accompaniments are often tabled like this:

Birmingham Jail

Where oh where Has My Little Dog Gone

Rests

A rest is not a note but a signature denoting a pause within the compass of a bar. Even though the rest is not played it is used in the same way as a note, and must be stopped for the total length of time specified.

To execute the rest, put the palm (heel) of your right hand across the strings for the exact amount of time specified by the rest sign.

For every note there is an equivalent rest sign:

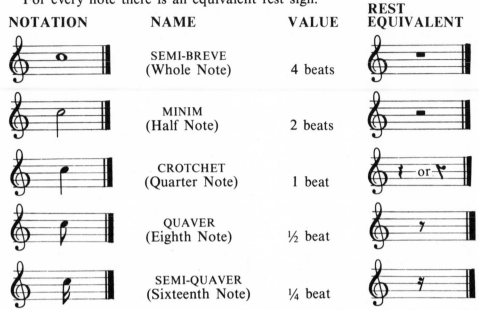

NOTATION	NAME	VALUE	REST EQUIVALENT
	SEMI-BREVE (Whole Note)	4 beats	
	MINIM (Half Note)	2 beats	
	CROTCHET (Quarter Note)	1 beat	or
	QUAVER (Eighth Note)	½ beat	
	SEMI-QUAVER (Sixteenth Note)	¼ beat	

Whenever a rest applies to a complete bar, the only rest sign that can be used (irrespective of the time signature) is the SEMI-BREVE (Whole Note) rest:

The Gypsy Baron

CHAPTER 7 # An Introduction to Composition, Expression and Notational Chords

The simplicity of music writing (composition)

The majority of music is written to strict patterns. Depending on the grading of the music, these patterns are generally simple. The far more complex harmonies that are often added to these simple patterns may at times obscure (or sound as if they have obscured) the simplicity of the melody line.

An excellent example of the simplicity of music formation and writing is the tune 'Little Polly Flinders':

Little Polly Flinders

The total context of this melody relies solely on six basic notes, C D E F G A. The notes are grouped in a pattern of one note to the next. The greatest gap is four notes apart, from D to G.

If it is realised that music is generally written in combinations of four bars, eight bars and sixteen bars (when written in common time), this tune can be broken down into two separate areas of eight bars each; and each eight-bar area can be further broken down into two separate areas of four bars each.

A closer inspection of bars 1 to 8 and bars 9 to 16 shows them to be of almost identical form, each having two separate melodies of four bars.

The first bar moves in the order G A G F to the second bar, which is the note E:

The second bar allows the third bar to begin on a note one alphabetical name higher than itself (E to F) and to follow the pattern of bars one and two, but one alphabetical name note lower in its alphabetical context:

The difference in structure between bars 1 to 4 and bars 9 to 12 is that phrasing changes in the tenth and twelfth bars have included two CROTCHET (Quarter Note) notes in place of the second MINIM (Half Note) note previously used in the second and fourth bars:

The distance between bars 4 and 5, and bars 12 and 13, is the greatest gap, being four notes from D to G. (It is interesting to observe that the note G is the opening note of each of the four four-bar sections.)

Bars 5 and 13 are identical, but bars 6 and 14 warrant further explanation. The different phrasing in these two bars illustrates how the use of different notation affects and facilitates the conclusions of each part.

Bar 6 leads to the conclusion of part one. The distance between its final note and bar 7 is the same as the gap between bars 4 and 5 (D to G). The note sequence in bar 6, leading to the note G, allows for repetition of the melody since G is the melody commencement (recommencement) note and leads itself through bars 7 and 8 to the introductory note of bar 9 (part two):

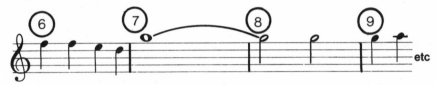

Bar 14 uses the same structure as bar 6, but omits the first CROTCHET (Quarter Note) note F, thus allowing for a pause effect from the MINIM (Half Note) note D before it ends on the key note of C. The pattern used for bars 14, 15 and 16 effectively ends the melody, and can easily be heard to do so, whereas the final three bars of part one help to maintain the effect and continuity of the melody concerned:

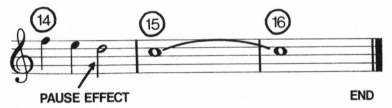

Pick-up notes (Anacrusis)

Pick-up notes, commonly known as a 'broken bar', are found when a certain accent of timing in relation to the melody cannot be fully written to occupy a bar in total. Under these circumstances, the first and last bar values are distributed accordingly, and the count begins in relation to the remaining notes of the first bar in a compensatory manner.

Oh when the Saints

Pebbles and Stones

Notes on the Fourth String

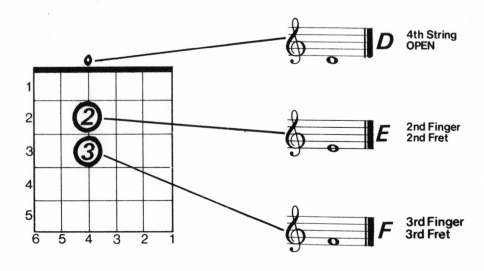

Fourth String Exercise

Fourth String Rock

Mama's Blues

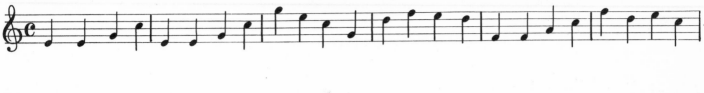

Dynamics in music

The dynamics in music occur as a mode of expression concerned with the relative intensity of performance. Simple examples and their symbols include:

p (piano) soft

pp (pianissimo) very soft

f (forte) loud

ff (fortissimo) very loud

Once the dynamic is applied it can govern the complete passage, or only part of the passage. You are usually expected to follow the stated dynamic expression mark until it alters, or until the structure of the music changes.

The dynamics also concern themselves with the accentation of music. The first beat of each bar is written in such a way that it will accent itself (hence the need for bar lines). If a specific, powerful accent is required for any reason, this may be shown by means of an attack sign (>)

Exercise with Dynamics and Attack Signs

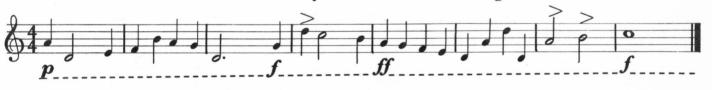

Little Brown Jug

The normal performance of 'Little Brown Jug' allows for an accent on the first beat of each bar. The accent in the last four bars is increased by the attack sign, which calls for an even greater emphasis on each of the accented beats.

The song is naturally a loud one, which accounts for the forte sign in the first four bars. Because the last four bars have their accent strengthened by the attack sign, it is advisable to write the passage in fortissimo so that the louder format, together with the attack sign, will greatly enhance the expression of the passage even though the notation is almost identical to the notation of the first four bars.

Chords

Any combination of a succession of notes played simultaneously is called a chord.

Chord Exercise No. 1

Triads

Any three notes written in a chord pattern are called a triad. The triad is a series of three notes written from the given notes of a specific scale (see page 63).

The triads on the following pages have been written for the first three strings of the guitar. They are based on chords that have already been studied earlier—see if you can recognise the chords being used.

Chord (Triad) Exercise No. 2

Three-String Chords

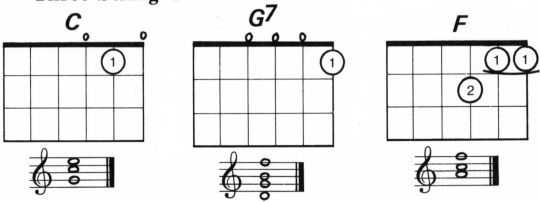

Chord (Three-String) Exercise No. 3

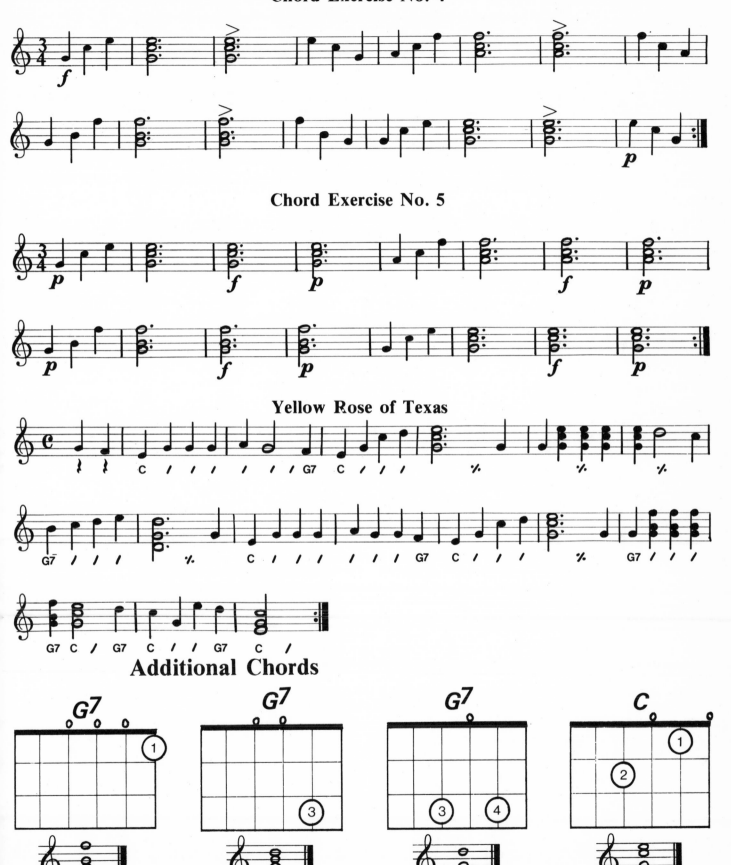

Chord Exercise No. 4

Chord Exercise No. 5

Yellow Rose of Texas

Additional Chords

55

Chord (Additional Chords) Exercise No. 6

Chord Exercise No. 7

Jingle Bells

Moderato

Moderato: This means that the whole passage is to be played at a moderate speed. If a metronome is being used to gauge the time value, apply the tempo at between 108 and 120 beats per minute.

The stem of a chord

The stem of a chord is written in much the same manner as the stem of a note (see page 43). The stem is written upwards or downwards depending on the notes within the chord, and the position they occupy on the staff. If most of the notes are above the third line, the stem is written downwards:

JINGLE BELLS bar1

If most of the notes are written below the third line, the stem must be written upwards:

JINGLE BELLS bar15

The stem can also be interchanged (written upwards or downwards) within the same bar if the music warrants it:

JINGLE BELLS bar 3 _ _ _ _ _ _ _ _ _ bar 7 _ _ _ _ _ _ _ _ _ _ _ bar 11

Beautiful Brown Eyes

Good Night Ladies

Allegro: The passage is to be played lively and fast (MM 120-168).

I've Been Working on the Railroad

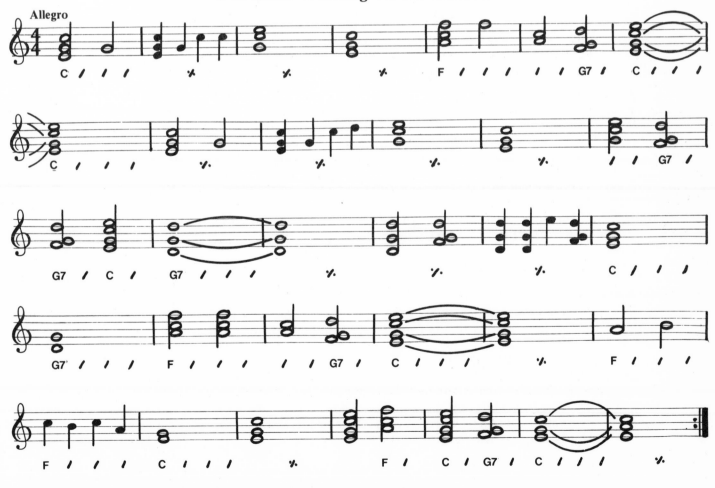

Further hints on tuning

Exact tunings are not easy to achieve at first. In order to tune correctly you must be aware of the pitch of the string you are tuning to the one already 'tuned'. If the 'tuned' string is tuned too high originally, you may tend to keep tuning higher and break the string.

You must be able to recognise immediately if a string is too high or too low so that you can adjust it accordingly.

If the note is being tuned from the fifth fret, and sounds incorrect, move up to the sixth, seventh, eighth or ninth frets, etc., until the exact unison pitch is obtained. If the pitch of the note is found above the fifth fret, the note is too low and therefore must be raised. Follow this progression until the exact unison pitch is obtained.

If moving beyond the fifth fret does not produce the exact pitch (or the notes continually sound too high) move below the fifth fret to the fourth, third, second, first or open frets until the identical pitch is obtained. If and when this pitch is found to be below the fifth fret, lower the tension of the string, continually checking its position by the two systems mentioned above, until the exact unison tuning is obtained.

When changing strings you may at times mistakenly tune them much higher than allowable. Check for this by using the two systems mentioned above. If no reasonable equivalent can be found by moving either upwards or downwards on the lower string (e.g., tuning the second string to the first string) begin fingering the higher string (first string) one fret at a time and play this against the open lower string (second string) until a reasonable equivalent pitch is found. If this pitch is duplicated on, say, the third fret of the higher string against the open lower string, immediately release the tension of the lower string because *it is tuned eight frets too high.* Then, and only then, check the pitch of the lower string by the methods previously described.

(Steel-strung guitars usually need about half a turn on the machine head to alter the string pitch by one fret. The nylon-strung guitar usually requires approximately one complete turn to alter its string pitch by one fret. Care should be taken at all times because these turns are approximates only and will vary from guitar to guitar depending on the 'cog capstan' and the individual 'string tensions'.)

Selecting tuning forks: Absolute care should be taken in the selection of tuning forks, for they will become an invaluable asset. Look after your tuning forks very carefully because they tend to become 'musically flat' rather quickly if abused.

Try to buy an E-320 or an A-440 tuning fork so that tuning can be done from the first string.

The tuning fork is best hit on the sole of the shoe, so that the blow may be cushioned. Hitting the fork on a really solid object can damage it since there is no cushioning effect.

Place the resonating tuning fork on the bridge of the guitar in order to amplify the sound. This creates a more distinct tone from which the string can be tuned.

The A-440 tuning fork is a little harder to become accustomed to than the E-320, for it means tuning from the fifth fret of the first string.

Playing solo guitar

Melodies are written consistently as guitar solos. This means that the music is harmonised in such a way that the guitar can be played by itself without any other instrument having to accompany it with chords, etc. Rhythmic and bass instruments can be included (at the performer's pleasure) in the solo structure of any music written as a guitar solo.

Symbols peculiar to the guitar

1 , 2 , 3 , 4   The number of the left-hand finger to be applied to the string(s).

②   The string on which the left-hand finger is to be placed.

3P ——————————   Left-hand 1st finger starts on the third fret, and each successive finger continues the formation one fret higher.

III · · · · · · · · · · · · · · · · · ·   Place the left-hand fingers in the Roman numeral position (III = third fret).

Maintain this position until the lines (or dots) stop.

C II   Barré (bar) with the left-hand 1st finger over all six strings.

½C II   Apply less than the six-string barré; can be used for a barré of two or more strings up to five strings.

The same as barré.

Slide the left-hand fingers upwards (along the neck) without sound.

Slide the left-hand fingers downwards (along the neck) without sound.

Run the plectrum slowly across the strings (bass to treble) to create a 'harp-roll' effect.

Ext 4   Extend the 4th finger to the note required and return immediately to its original position.

Maintain left-hand fingering of notes.

CHAPTER 8 Scales, Tetrachords, Keys and Chord Construction within Scales

Notes on the Fifth String

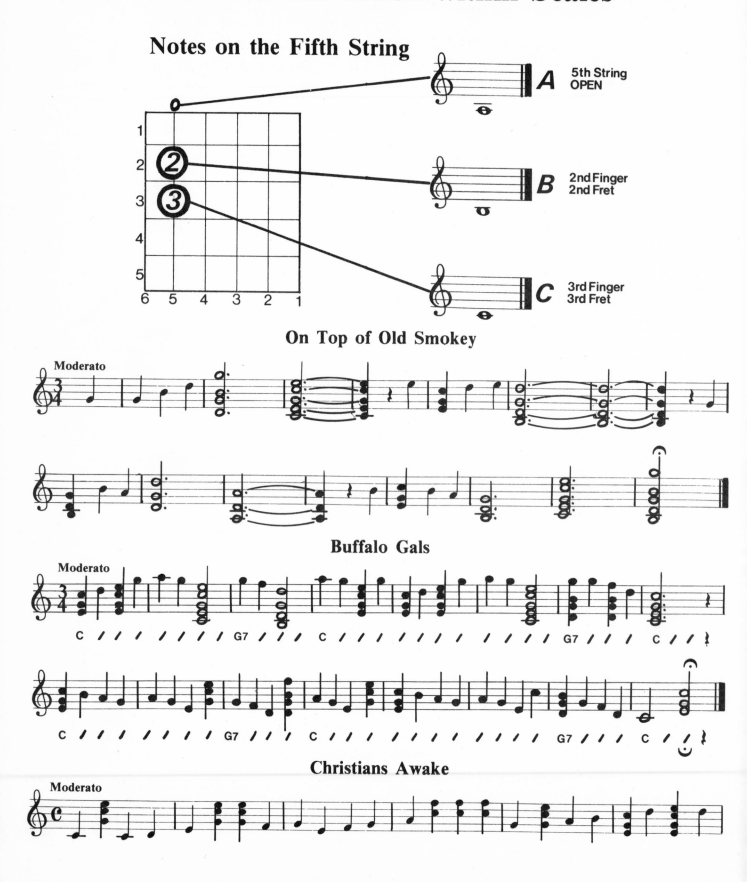

A — 5th String OPEN

B — 2nd Finger 2nd Fret

C — 3rd Finger 3rd Fret

On Top of Old Smokey

Moderato

Buffalo Gals

Moderato

Christians Awake

Moderato

The scale

The scale is a logical series of notes combining themselves in a specific pattern suitable for harmony. Although there are many 'scales and modes' the most common of these, in use today, is the *major scale*. Its internal character is based on the movements of *tones* and *semi-tones* (English terminology) or *whole steps* and *half steps* (American terminology).

TONE   (T) Notes written *two* frets apart (whole step).

SEMI-TONE   (ST) Notes written *one* apart (half step).

Tetrachords

The scale can be best described by using the word tetrachord (from the Greek 'tetra', meaning four, and the Latin 'chorda'); it consists of a series of four successive notes written to a given pattern:

The most common tetrachord formula is the one used above:

TONE,   TONE,   SEMI-TONE
(WHOLE STEP),   (WHOLE STEP),   (HALF STEP)

Whenever two successive tetrachords are written ascending, they are placed one tone (one whole step) apart and form the basis of the major scale. Each individual note is called a *degree*.

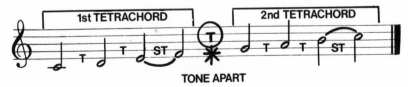

The major scale is not usually written with the tetrachord 'capitals' shown, but follows the style set out below:

MAJOR SCALE FORMULA

FIRST TETRACHORD	1st to 2nd degree 2nd to 3rd degree 3rd to 4th degree	TONE TONE SEMI-TONE	(WHOLE STEP) (WHOLE STEP) (HALF STEP)
TONE APART	4th to 5th degree	TONE	(WHOLE STEP)
SECOND TETRACHORD	5th to 6th degree 6th to 7th degree 7th to 8th degree	TONE TONE SEMI-TONE	(WHOLE STEP) (WHOLE STEP) (HALF STEP)

Scale Study

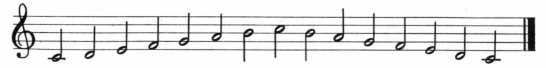

Speed Study No. 1

Speed Study No. 2

Degrees of a scale

This is a functional method of naming the individual notes of a scale, either by numerals or specific names. It is particularly useful in the harmonic analysis of music because the degree names can take in (and explain) the total compass of scales without the use of complex notation.

1st degree	TONIC	The name of the note after which the key or scale is named.
2nd degree	SUPER-TONIC	The note directly above the tonic note.
3rd degree	MEDIANT	The note midway between the tonic and the 5th degree.
4th degree	SUB-DOMINANT	The note directly below the dominant note. (If the scale were reversed, this degree would become the 5th degree, with the same interval as the dominant.)
5th degree	DOMINANT	Due to the strong harmonic influence of this note it dominates the sound of the key being used. (*Note:* The dominant degree supports the dominant 7th chord of any given key.)
6th degree	SUB-MEDIANT	The note midway between the sub-dominant and tonic degrees; it also falls in direct reverse to the mediant degree.
7th degree	LEADING NOTE	Through its progression this leads to the tonic note. (It also serves as the strong note of the 7th chord and the link-note of further chord progressions, such as the 9th chord, etc. The strong dominating factor of this note is always used in the dominant chord of any key.)
8th degree	UPPER-TONIC	One octave above the tonic note, or the note after which the key is named. (Also referred to as the link-note of an extended octave, since it serves as the 1st and 8th degree of any scale.)

The chord

Whenever three or more notes are struck simultaneously they are called a chord. The nature of the chord can take many shapes and forms, but the most common chord is the major chord.

The major chord can be written directly from its tonic scale by extracting the 1st, 3rd and 5th degrees:

SCALE OF C MAJOR

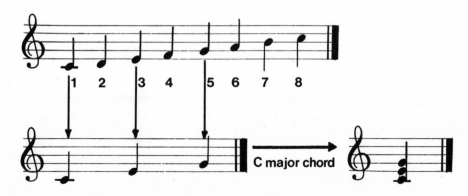

C major chord

The C major chord consists of three basic scale notes:

*C *E *G

Whatever the combination applied in writing these notes in music, they will always form the C major chord. However, as the notes change sequence so does their rudimentary name.

ROOT POSITION	FIRST INVERSION	SECOND INVERSION
1 – 3 – 5	3 – 5 – 1	5 – 1 – 3

Because the guitar has a minimum (open string) span of two octaves, it is not uncommon to write the chord duplicating notation (in combinations of inversions) while relying heavily on each of the inversions for the required note(s) to be applied with a chordal backing:

CONTINUAL COMBINATIONS OF INVERSIONS

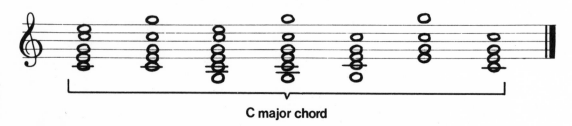

C major chord

The key

There are three principal chords within any given key:

TONIC CHORD based on the 1st scale degree
SUB-DOMINANT CHORD based on the 4th scale degree
DOMINANT CHORD based on the 5th scale degree

The major scale can within itself produce the three principal chords of the key. Furthermore, these basic chords appear within its total contents.
Tonic chord: Obtain the tonic note and ascend by two 3rds. Scale degrees 1 – 3 – 5.

Sub-dominant chord: Obtain the upper-tonic note, and descend by two 3rds. Scale degrees 8 – 6 – 4.

Dominant chord: Use the internal notes of either the tonic or sub-dominant chords and ascend or descend by two 3rds. Scales degrees are from the internal tonic 5 – 7 – 2 – 4, or from the internal note of the sub-dominant 4 – 2 – 7 – 5.

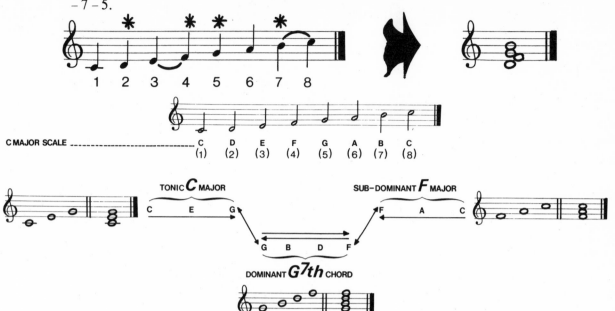

C MAJOR SCALE ------------------------------ C   D   E   F   G   A   B   C
                                            (1) (2) (3) (4) (5) (6) (7) (8)

Therefore the **key of C major** consists of three basic chords:

TONIC	C MAJOR	C E G
SUB-DOMINANT	F MAJOR	F A C
DOMINANT	G7 (seventh)	G B D F

Key C Boogie

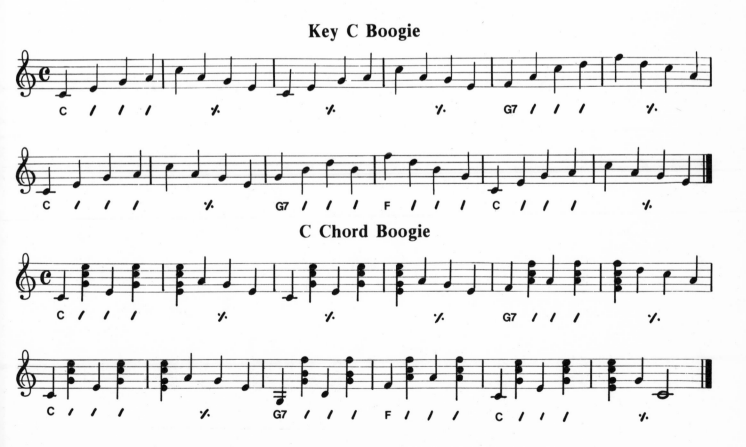

C Chord Boogie

Dashing through the Snow

Sing a Song of Sixpence

My Bonnie

Red River Valley

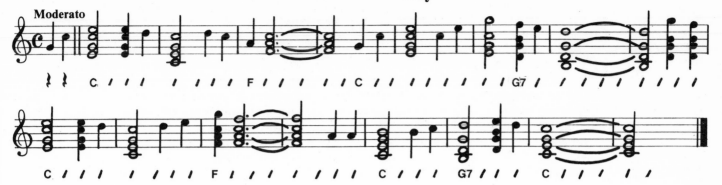

Alternate method of tuning the guitar

Another method of tuning the guitar is directly from the piano key-board.

If it is remembered that the notes of the guitar are written one octave higher than the true (playable) pitch, the first and second strings can be tuned starting around middle C on the piano in unisons; the remainder can then be tuned to almost two octaves below the middle C area in unisons.

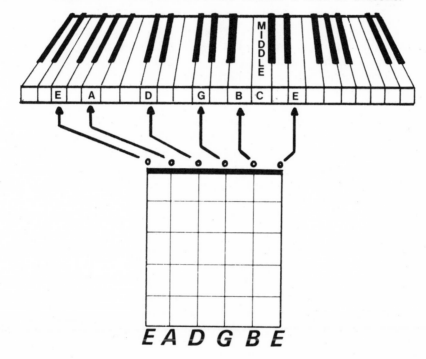

E A D G B E

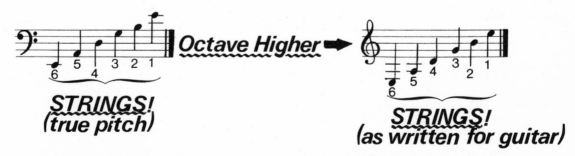

It is important that the notes be taken from their true piano equivalents in unison, for neither the strings nor the guitar will take the additional pressure of one octave. If the over-tuned strings do not break, the instrument could be badly damaged.

Tensioning of strings

If you have a nylon-strung guitar, you will find it rather difficult to tune the instrument after changing the strings, for they will keep lowering their pitch. Because of this pitch problem, corrective measures such as tensioning the strings should be used.

Certain 'don'ts' that should be appreciated when attempting tensioning:
(1) *Do not tune the instrument higher than the accepted concert pitch and allow the strings to stretch to the required tone.* Overall higher tension on the guitar could permanently damage the instrument, especially the body, for the guitar is built to maximum pressure points. Abuse this and a multitude of problems could occur. NEVER tune the instrument higher than its allowable pitch.

(2) *Do not allow the instrument to settle into its own tensioned pitch over a period of time.* This will lead to constant re-tuning (even when playing) for up to a period of one month. By that time the strings will probably be badly worn and in need of replacement.

Furthermore, if this method is continually employed, you will probably never be able to appreciate the correct pitching of the notes (so vital to your progression).

(3) *Do not release the tension of the strings after each practice.* This can put a multitude of different pressures on the instrument, and can damage it in the process. Nor does this method permit the strings to reach their correct tension, and the guitar will remain permanently out of tune both physically and harmonically.

The correct way to obtain proper tension:
Tension your strings by stretching. Gently lift the strings (use your right hand above the 'nut') to release any built-up tension, at the same time periodically tugging the strings with additional pressure. As the string is being tensioned, the right hand gradually progresses (tugging the strings) along the frets while holding the string above the nut as far as possible.

After the first tension re-tune the string to its concert pitch (it will probably be in excess of one octave lower than this required pitch) and continue the process, always retuning the guitar after each tensioning, until the stretch is almost no more than one fret in movement.

The machine head may have to be turned as many as twenty or thirty times during this process to realise the full stretch potential. Do not let this amount of stretch worry you unduly, for it is normal with this type of string.[1]

After completing the first tension it is advisable to re-tension within half an hour. This will re-adjust the tension of each string and will also make it easier to maintain the concert pitch of the guitar (allowing for normal tuning adjustments at any later stage) until the next change of strings.

The above method can also be applied—extremely cautiously—to the lighter gauge steel strings of the plectrum guitar. To tension these strings do not use your fingers (they can be cut by the very thin strings) but a smooth, strong object such as a ball-point pen.

---

1 The pupil who over-tunes his guitar to obtain the same effect as tensioning should now appreciate the inadequacies of that method. If the guitar was originally over-tuned, he will find that after tensioning his strings will become higher in pitch and tend to return to the over-tensioned pitch to which the strings have become accustomed. It will take quite some time for the guitar strings to settle down to the required pitch and to maintain sounds without continually returning to the higher, pre-tuned pitch.

Vigorous tensioning to restore the concert pitch—from the higher pitch—could then permanently damage the strings, thus rendering them harmonically useless with the possibility of the overtones on the strings resulting in more than one note being played simultaneously.

CHAPTER 9 # The True Compass of Guitar Pitching

Leger lines

Leger lines are small lines placed above or below the staff whenever its compass cannot accommodate the independent pitch required (above or below the available pitch area).

The pitching of the leger lines can be shown far more clearly by the use of the Great Stave, a device used during the Middle Ages and applied in recent times to explain more fully the compass of musical notation.

The great stave consisted of eleven staff lines and ten spaces. As the centre line of the great stave was omitted, two separate clef areas emerged: the treble (G) clef $\oint$ and the bass (F) clef $\mathbf{\mathfrak{I}}$. The centre line was called 'C', and was the origin of the middle C line of the piano-forte[2] clef.

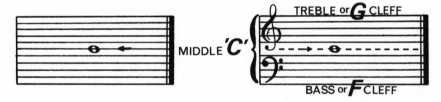

Great Stave   **Piano-Forte Stave**

The leger lines can be clearly seen emerging from the fifth and sixth strings of the guitar fingerboard, and its total compass is written as follows:

The pupil must at all times treat his instrument with caution. Constant abuse, caused by ignorance or pseudo-expert advice, is a very common occurrence among beginners. The instrument is a frail one, and must be treated accordingly. If the pupil requires any advice an expert should be consulted, for only an expert is best able to advise—in detail—on the problems of the style of instrument concerned.

2 Piano-forte music: As its name ('soft-loud') suggests, this music was originally written for the organ, still the only manual instrument capable of great variety in its dynamics from soft to loud. Modern usage classifies piano-forte music as 'piano' music, and various schools of thought imply that the piano was the original piano-forte musical instrument, although the piano is only about 200 years old. The combined piano-forte stave was in use long before that, and the only instruments then capable of being played in this manner were those of the harpsichord family and the organ—but the harpsichord is widely known for its soft, romantic sound, and is inherently incapable of living up to the full meaning of piano-forte. The organ has survived for more than 400 years, and although it relies on bellows and pipes in contrast to the hammers of the piano, the notation of both the organ and piano key-boards is identical.

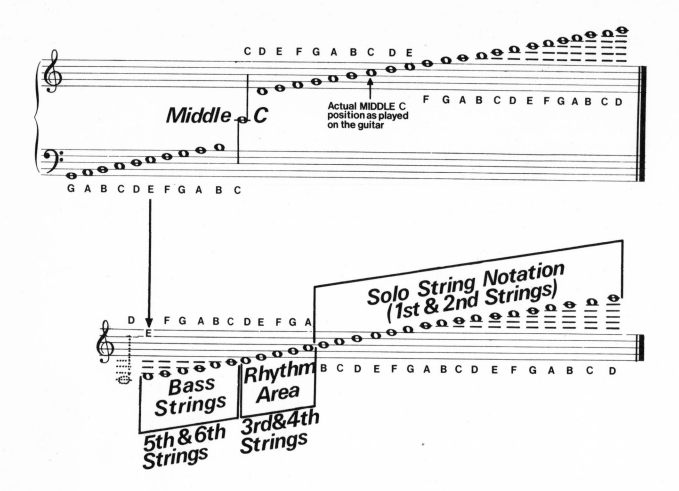

It should be noted that the guitar is sometimes tuned as low as the note D on the sixth string. This note is one tone lower than the range of regular 'Spanish tuning', thus allowing a greater range of notation and giving the plectrum guitar a ratio of up to four octaves.

As the inclusion of the leger lines from the bass clef to the treble clef stops at the middle C note, this area can be taken as the 'bass production' area of the guitar. It perfectly encompasses the sixth and fifth strings.

If the centre line of the treble clef were used as a means of determining the 'solo area' (reversed to the centre line of the bass clef) this would then encompass the second and first strings.

The remaining fourth and third strings can be termed the 'rhythmic area', since they fall between middle C and the centre treble clef line.

Although the system of gauging the separate strings (in pairs) in terms of bass, rhythm and solo playing is idealistic, it is often used as a guide to the guitar compass by classical and jazz guitarists. The system is optional, and may be strictly adhered to, interchanged or expanded at the pleasure of the performer or arranger.

Pitching of the guitar

Even though the guitar has a compass of up to four octaves (the nylon-strung model is usually of three and a half octaves) it is written an octave lower than its true reproductive sound. Therefore the guitar is played one octave higher than it is written.

This form of transposition is applied to avoid the unnecessary inclusion of two separate clef signs, even though the guitar is capable of playing more than two separate lines of music (as with right- and left-hand piano arrangements) at the same time.

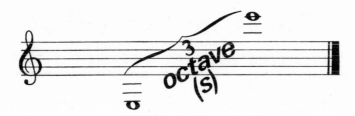

Notation is occasionally used as far as the twelfth fret (E) of the first string, but rarely above this area. Therefore the treble clef is ideal since it offers three leger lines either side of its compass for all 'normal' and 'extreme' areas of performance.

The three octaves are the accepted usual maximum range of the guitar in performance capability, and the writing of music in its true pitch would tend to confuse, rather than maintain simplicity in the production of its music.

It is also of interest that the guitar has a range only one octave smaller than that of the organ key-board, without the foot-pedal range in one voicing. The additional voicings on the organ allow for a hearing capacity that sounds far greater than it actually is. Guitar voicings can also be expanded immeasurably by the use of harmonics (see page 115), since these can be played beyond the hearing capacity of the human ear.

The piano key-board contains a total of seven octaves within its compass. **The true compass of the guitar** has been written below, using both clefs, to make you aware of the difficulty of the reading in this form (since only one hand is used—not two as with key-board instruments). The bass strings would in fact involve leger lines to eight lines below the treble clef in its true pitch.

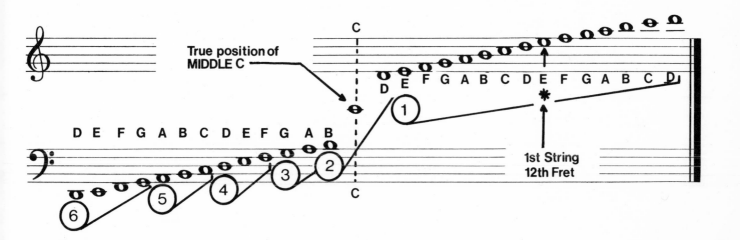

Polyphony, Technical Development and Dodecaphonics

Notes on the Sixth String

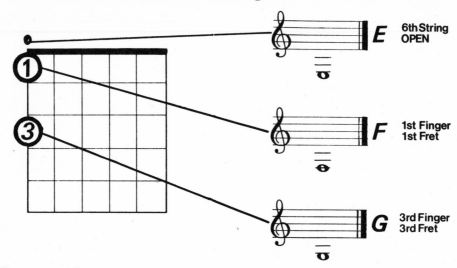

Down and up strokes on the guitar

The use of both down and up strokes is not uncommon with the guitar.

Although all of the pieces you have so far played have used down strokes, greater speed and fluency will be obtained if the two styles are combined for a speed study.

The most common method is the rotating *down ... up ... down ... up ...* etc. This helps fix the position of the right-hand wrist so that maximum control is obtained with minimum effort.

⊓ DOWN STROKE

V UP STROKE

Simile: This means 'maintain the same progression with the right hand for the remaining bars, unless otherwise stated'.

Speed Study No. 3

The G7th chord

One of the most interesting and versatile chords (in the open position) is the G7th chord.

The setting of the chord notes (G B D F) encompasses three open strings, and the remainder of the notes can be found within two tones (two whole steps) of the open notes.

The seemingly endless combinations of fingers and notes make for exciting expression, and will prove invaluable for harmonisation at a later stage.

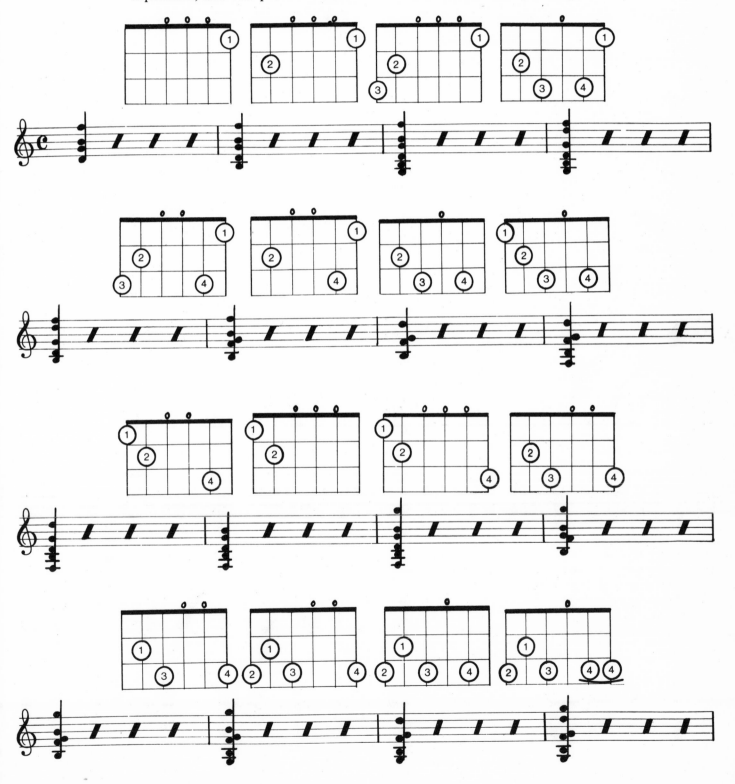

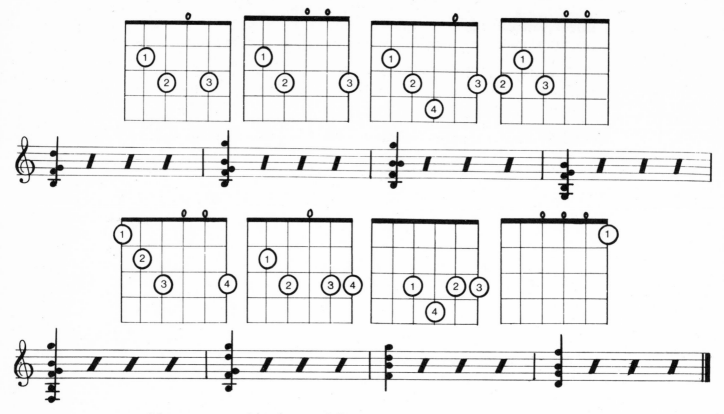

Many more combinations and finger patterns can be written. Those shown here offer you an approach to progressive fingering, thus limiting the movement of the left hand, and will also sharpen your appreciation and awareness of the chord and the elementary fingerboard.

Camptown Races

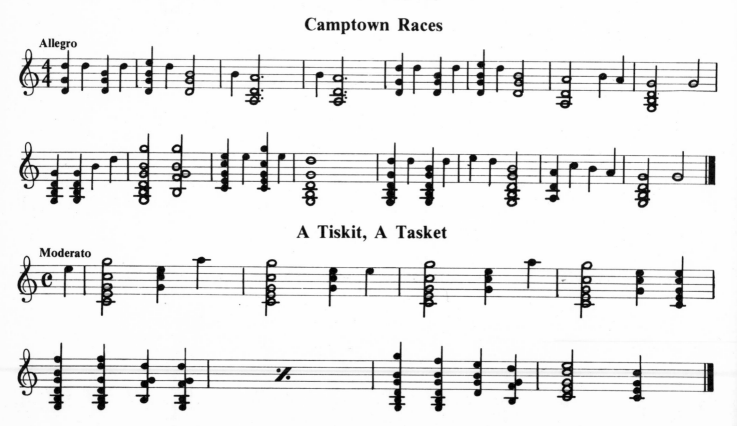

A Tiskit, A Tasket

This melody is usually played at a much faster pace, but moderato has been specified here because of the difficult fingering in the last four bars.

Fantasy Time

Reading two lines of music for the guitar (polyphonic)

It is possible to write more than one line of music, within the same clef, to be played by the one instrument. This allows the performer to read both bass and solo or rhythm and solo; or rhythm and bass parts simultaneously. The polyphonic style can also successfully lengthen harmonies of passages while a continuous solo or bass line is being played against them.

Whenever the two lines combine, the note stem follows the specified passage. The top line notes are always stemmed upwards, and the lower line notes always carry the stem downwards.

To the untrained musician there would appear to be too much notation within the one bar. In fact, the total notation will be exactly double that of the time signature. You must therefore be aware of the structure of the music being written as two separate performers would play it, thus accounting for the duplication of the total combined value of the bar beats.

In the following example, two separate lines (separate voices) are written, with the explanatory combined two-line style directly below:

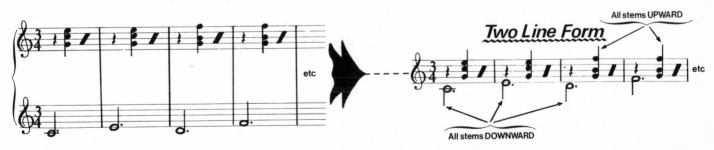

The DOTTED MINIM (Dotted Half Note) written in the lower part is played on the count of one and held for the counts of two and three. The CROTCHET (Quarter Note) beats of the upper area are played on the beats of two and three only. The first beat is a CROTCHET (Quarter Note) rest, thus allowing for the uninterrupted playing of the first beat of the lower part.

Points of interest in two-line (polyphonic) music: As with the upward or the downward stemming of notation (irrespective of the staff position), all rest positions must also be altered so as not to confuse the performer about which line they belong to.

Although it would be impossible to maintain the rest in exact positions—due to the fluctuations of music—the recommended areas are:

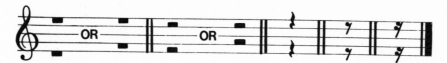

If the structure of the music will not allow for this form of placement, the required rests should then be extended to the extremes of, or beyond, the compass of the staff:

The placing of a dot to the right-hand side of a dotted note remains unaltered for the upward stem. If the note falls on a staff space, the dot is written directly behind it. But if the note falls on a staff line, the dot follows it on the space area directly above the line:

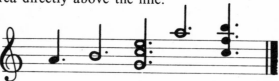

The dot for the downward stem of staff space notes is placed in the same way as for the upward stem, but for downward stem line notes the dots must always be written in the space directly below:

The orchestration stroke can still be applied, but only if the music is written simply enough, and only so long as the line to which it belongs is easily recognised. Unfortunately the position of the orchestration stroke is fixed, and cannot be readily adjusted as is the case with rests.

(Correct)

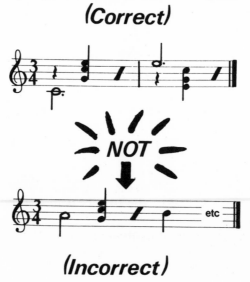

(Incorrect)

Walse Poco
(Single Line Form)

Presto: To be played very fast (MM 168-200). Although it is marked presto,
'Walse Poco' should be thoroughly studied at first (in the preparatory stage)
and should now be played slowly until you can handle the correct tempo.

Walse Poco
(Dual Line Form)

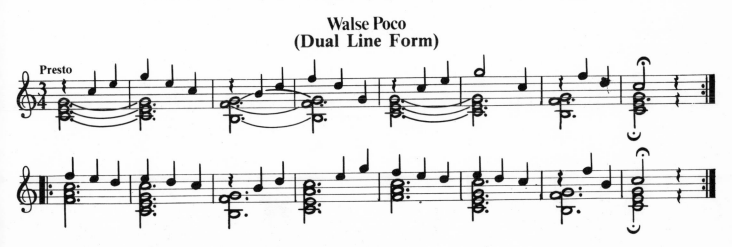

Au Clair de la Lune

Andante: To be played at an easy walking pace (MM 76-108).

Slumber Time

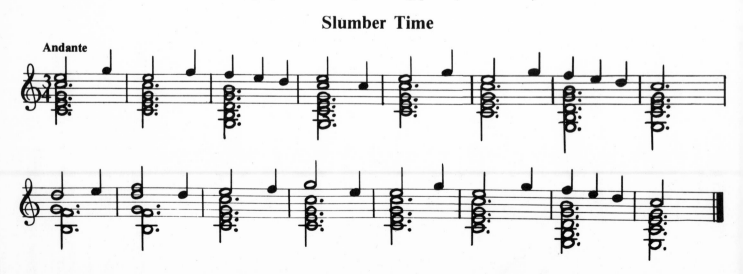

Go tell Aunt Rhodie

Deadened notes

When the guitar is being played, certain harmonies are required for effect—but, as is often the case, either there are not enough fingers available, or the position selected will not allow for the total inclusion of chordal notes in an arranged fingering suitable for the guitar.

Each example below suffers from 'not enough fingers'.

To deaden any required note, simply allow the left-hand finger (of the lower string) to stop the sound by bending onto the adjacent string without pressure.

Skip to My Loo

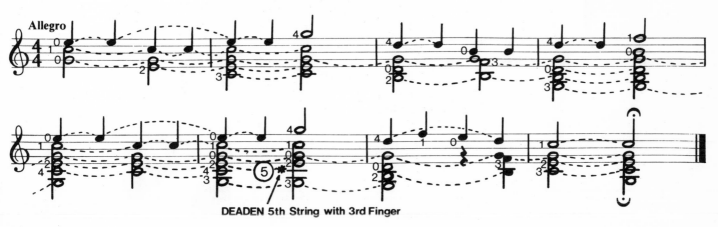

DEADEN 5th String with 3rd Finger

Sur le Pont d'Avignon

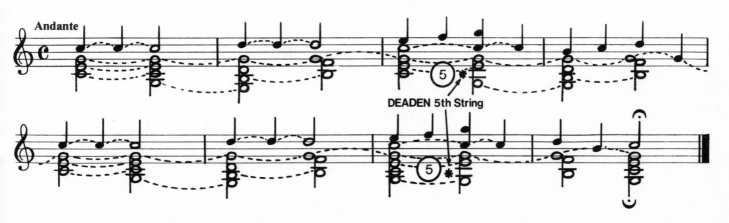

DEADEN 5th String

Blue Tail Fly

Accidentals

An accidental is a sign indicating the momentary raising or lowering of the pitch of any note not found within the key signature.

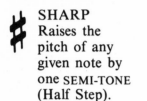 **SHARP** Raises the pitch of any given note by one SEMI-TONE (Half Step).

♭ **FLAT** Lowers the pitch of any given note by one SEMI-TONE (Half Step).

♮ **NATURAL** Restores the note to its original pitch, cancelling the effect of any previous sharp or flat.

When an accidental is applied to any note it will control all notes of that pitch (irrespective of octave placement) throughout the bar, unless otherwise cancelled by another accidental.

It is not unusual for 'reminder accidentals' to be placed in brackets within a specified bar (especially if the octave changes) and for the composer or arranger to reinstate that particular note (by a natural sign) in the following bar, although the measure of the previous bar (bar line) has cancelled the effective control the accidental sign had over that note.

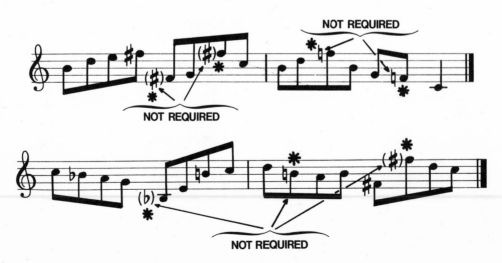

Chromatic scale (dodecaphonic)

The chromatic or dodecaphonic scale is a means of combining the notational forms of all available major scales. The chromatic scale is graded in twelve steps of semi-tones, and its diatonic range is thirteen notes.

The two types of explanatory chromatic scales are:

ASCENDING TO IMPLEMENT SHARPS
Semi-tones (half steps)

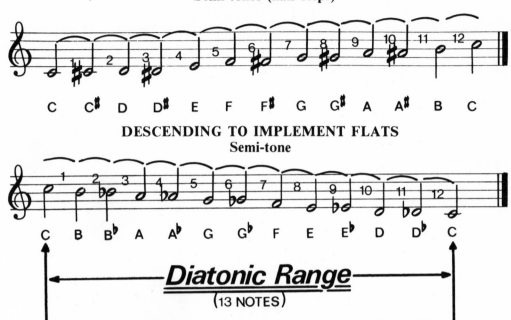

DESCENDING TO IMPLEMENT FLATS
Semi-tone

Enharmonic notation

Enharmonics occur whenever two notes of the same pitch have different names allocated to them. The chromatic scales above are enharmonic to each other if both are ascending or descending at the one time.

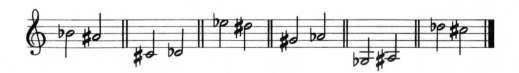

ENHARMONIC TO   Each ENHARMONIC note shares the same position of 1st String, 2nd Fret

Other enharmonics are:

OPEN POSITION CHROMATIC RANGE OF SHARPS

Left-hand development exercise through use of the open position chromatic range

As each finger of the left hand is applied to the guitar, it is kept in that position until it is needed for a note on a higher string. All other fingers are kept on the notes previously played until needed again.

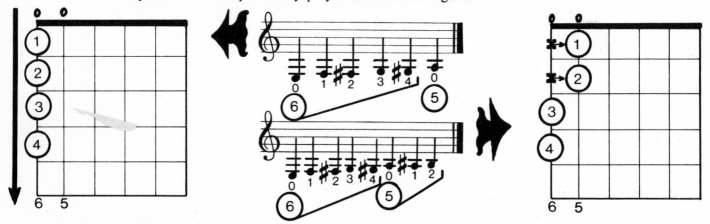

Whenever one finger is placed on a required position it must remain unaltered in that position (maintaining full pressure) until moved to a higher string.

It is of the utmost importance that the left hand be correctly placed from the first note, for a progression of fingers (including open strings) will not allow higher notation to resonate due to the incorrect curvature of the fingertips.

Practise this formula until the fourth fret of the first string is reached with all fingers firmly placed on the four frets of the first string.

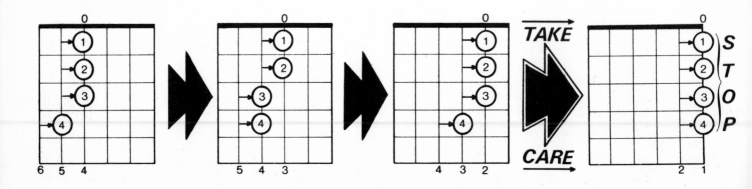

LEFT-HAND DEVELOPMENT ASCENDING

MAINTAIN PLACE—MENT OF FINGERS UNTIL MOVED TO A HIGHER STRING

As the four fingers are held tightly along the first string, in the four separate frets concerned, begin to descend (chromatically in flats) by maintaining the position of each finger and, as a further note is required, lift the finger concerned from the fingerboard and immediately replace it in the adjacent fret of its lower string.

You will notice that the note B (open second string) and its unison note B (4th finger, fourth fret, third string) are both applied in the development exercises. This placement is to be preferred for the correct development of the left hand, rather than the following chromatic form and only using the B in its open or closed unison.

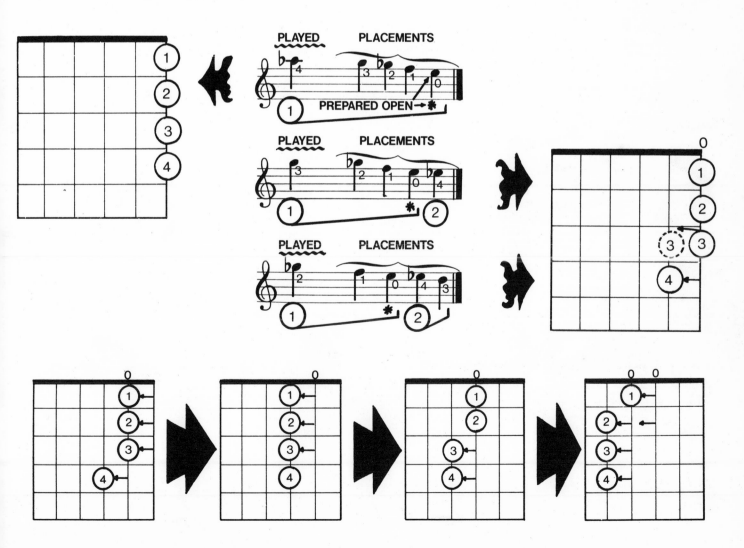

The descending tract leading to (and into) the sixth string allows for the individual fingers to be removed one at a time, thus reversing the starting process.

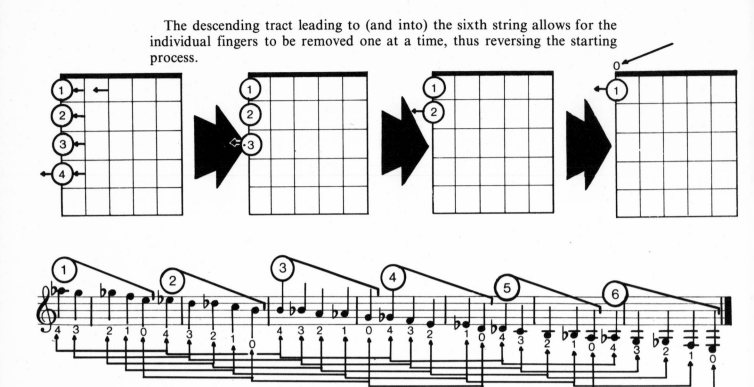

Practise the above exercises slowly at least once each day. The faster the passage is performed, the less will muscular development be achieved, and consequently many mistakes will go unnoticed.

Play the total ascending and descending areas at the one time, realising that it is important to complete the total exercise—irrespective of pains in the wrist—if the full benefit is to be obtained.

Dark Eyes

Sharps Galore

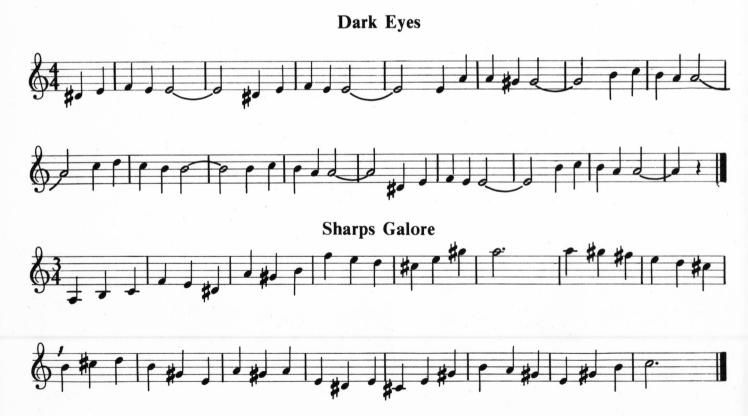

Preparing for each lesson: You should make sure that the work you allocate yourself (or the work allocated by your teacher) is done on a scheduled basis from one week to the next.

To help prepare yourself for the next lesson:

(1) Check your hand and sitting positions before starting to play. If necessary, use a mirror to see if they correspond with the diagrams on pages 25, 26 and 27

(2) Approach each practice session carefully. Take into consideration the speed and accuracy demanded by each piece. It is much more important to develop correctly than to go for speed at this point.

Playing by touch: Watching either hand while you are playing will mean constant loss of timing and of your position in the music you are reading.

If your control is incorrect, attempt to play by touch rather than by observation. This method is within everyone's reach, and easily allows for the desired control to be applied.

Even more importantly it will let you concentrate further on your timing and enable you to correct any deficiencies that may be apparent.

Minimise finger movement: Always finger the shortest possible distance between any two chords, for the greater the movement of your left hand the greater the time involved in changing chords.

If your left-hand thumb is applied correctly—not protruding above the neck—you will find it easier to minimise your finger movements.

Application of daily exercises: A few carefully chosen exercises can be of far more value than the constant repetition of practised pieces. If you don't have time for a full practice, use what time you do have for exercises. Although you may feel that your playing has not progressed for that one day, your muscular and hand control will at least remain intact.

Use of the capo: The capo (*cap a'dastro*) is an ancient device used to shorten the length of the available string vibration and consequently raise the pitch of the instrument.

The experienced guitarists will avoid the use of this object. The finger barre will more than compensate, while at the same time allowing the hand to move freely over the fingerboard. The only real exceptions are flamenco guitarists who rarely have enough fingers for the passages they play and who rely heavily on the natural (open string) keys in position.

Unfortunately the capo, as used by most performers, tends to restrict both fingers and knowledge. This is common among the 'folk guitarists' who have only a limited knowledge of chord positions.

The capo should be avoided by the sincere student. If you do use it, use it preferably on only the second, fourth and seventh frets since they are the least harmonically affected areas of the guitar fingerboard.

Additional relevant musical terms:

Accelerando (accel) gradually becoming faster
Rallentando (rall) gradually becoming slower
Ritardando (ritard) gradually becoming slower
Ritenuto (rit) immediately slower or held back
A tempo return to former speed

Crescendo (cres) gradually becoming louder
Decrescendo gradually becoming softer
Diminuendo (dim) gradually becoming softer

Legato smoothly, well connected
Staccato detached, short

PART THREE
Graduated arrangements and expanded musicology

CHAPTER 11

Additional Timing and Octave Tuning

The quaver (eighth note) beat

Each QUAVER (Eighth Note) note receives a total count of half a beat; or two QUAVERS (Eighth Notes) are equal to one CROTCHET (Quarter Note) and are applied at each foot tap.

The note can be shown as a flag added to the stem ♪ , or can be joined to additional QUAVER notes by a heavy line at the end of each stem ♫

Whenever the QUAVER occurs you must automatically learn to think in terms of twice the number of notes you would consider in counting for CROTCHET timing. The foot still only taps to the CROTCHET beat, but timing is also applied to the upward foot movement, giving double the output for the required timing.

Each note previously studied still maintains its total time value, but is now counted in terms of QUAVER beat timing.

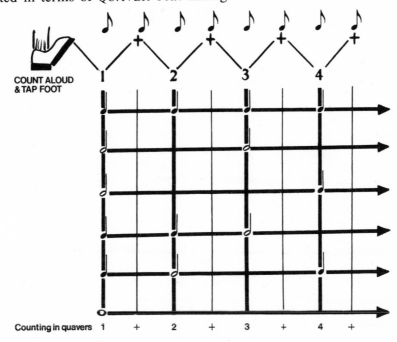

Counting in quavers 1 + 2 + 3 + 4 +

Alternatively, you may wish to associate each note in its total value with the QUAVER (Eighth Note).

Whichever method is applied, the count for $\frac{4}{4}$ remains 'one and two and three and four and . . .'; and the count for $\frac{3}{4}$ remains 'one and two and three and . . .'.

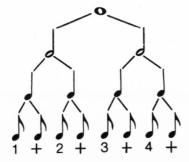

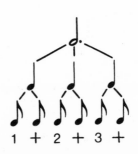

C Scale Study

Speed Study No. 4

Waltzing Matilda

Silent Night

Polly Wolly Doodle

Octave tuning

One of the more accurate methods of tuning is tuning by octaves. The musician tunes the guitar in a ratio of octaves, in either one or two octave scale variances.

The following octave ratios are only a guide, and you may wish to incorporate a far more complex octave pattern—one which better suits your hearing and fingering.

Obtain the sound of the first string (E) by means of a constant pitch, using your ear if it is suitably developed at this stage.

Tune the second string (B) in octave to the seventh fret (B) of the first string, the first string B being exactly one octave higher than the pitch of the second string.

The third string (G) is one octave above the third fret (G) of the first string.

The fourth string (D) is one octave above the D note of the second string.

The fifth string (A) to the fifth fret (A) of the first string is a distance of two octaves.

The sixth string (E) to the first string (E) is a distance of two octaves.

Unless your ear is sufficiently developed, octave tuning can present problems. So, at first, try octave tuning only after unison tuning as a means of double checking the exactness of the previously tuned instrument.

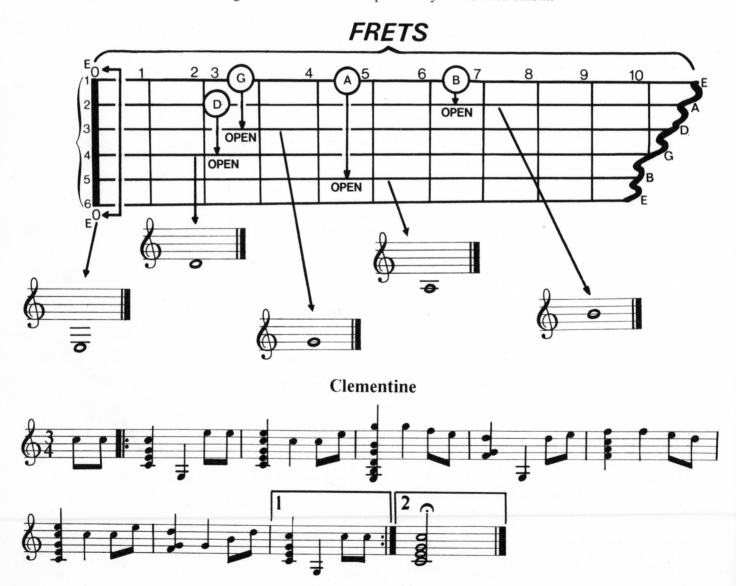

Clementine

90

Swing Low, Sweet Chariot

CHAPTER 12 # Key Signatures, Cycle of Accidentals and Intervals

The key signature

The key signature is an academic, tablature-style analysis of the form a musical composition will take. Within its character it will not only direct the performer to the required key of the melody but will also indicate the notational structure to be taken by the music and the number of accidentals that may be required during the playing.

The most common way of showing the key signature is through the **cycle of accidentals**, moving clockwise in scale 5ths and anti-clockwise in scale 4ths:

Each separate key signature has its allocation of relevant accidentals—peculiar to that key in its major and relative minor—which are in fixed positions, and which will not alter in form until a further key change is required by the composer.

Although the cycle of accidentals is satisfactory in showing the key signatures by their individual positions, it leaves much to be desired regarding the simplicity with which key signatures may be written for a particular musical passage.

This system of tetrachords written in the ascending form shows more clearly the development of the position of notation in the construction of key signatures:

TETRACHORD FORMULATION OF SHARPS

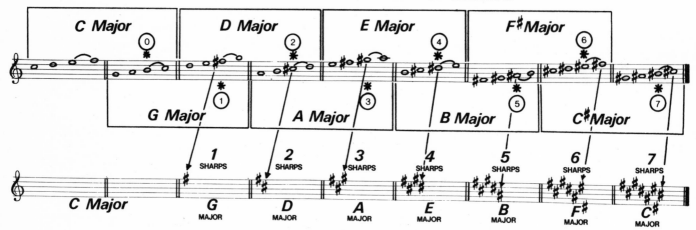

Each tetrachord creates a new scale (as an overlap of the previous scale) and in turn shows the positioning of the accidentals in sharps.

The sharps are formed by continually placing tetrachords as high as possible within this compass. Notation cannot be written below the immediate staff, nor can it be written above the note one leger line above the staff.

Each additional tetrachord 3rd degree will form the additional required accidental, and consequently the new key signature, of the overlapping tetrachord in its scale form. In turn, each additional accidental is written in a fixed position so that similarity and continuity can be maintained.

The above examples show the scale of E major written in three separate octaves, with the key signature remaining constant in its fixed position.

English Trilogy

The British Grenadiers
John Peel
There is a Tavern in the Town

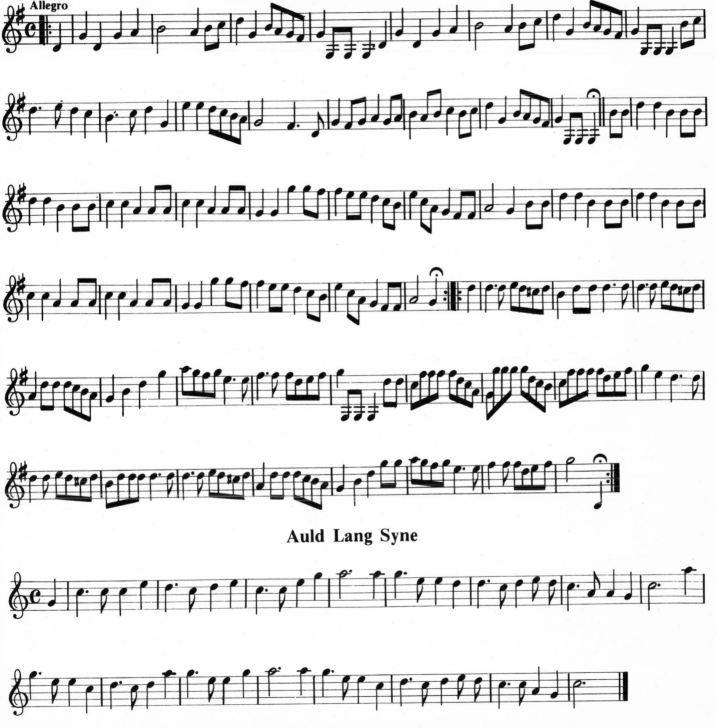

Auld Lang Syne

The formation of the key signatures in flats is the reverse of the placement of the tetrachord formulation of sharps:

TETRACHORD FORMULATION OF FLATS

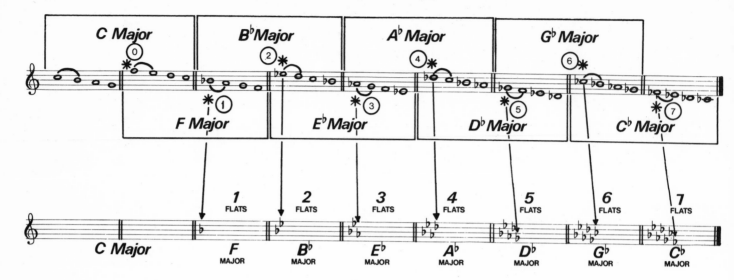

All tetrachords are now written in a descending motion (reversing the position of the tetrachord), thus creating an accidental on the opposite side of the semi-tone area of the tetrachord.

Furthermore, it should be noted that there is also a direct contrast between the placement of the notes within the staff. Notes cannot be written higher than the compass of the staff, nor can any note be written lower than the leger line note directly below the staff (C♭).

Again, all notes have a fixed position, and are added to by each additional position of the added accidental.

Further proof of the simplicity of music, and of its minimal requirements, is that the alphabetical sequence of each flat key signature is the reverse of that of the sharps.

FLATS _____ B♭ – E♭ – A♭ – D♭ – G♭ – C♭ – F♭

SHARPS _____ F♯ – C♯ – G♯ – D♯ – A♯ – E♯ – B♯

Row your Boat

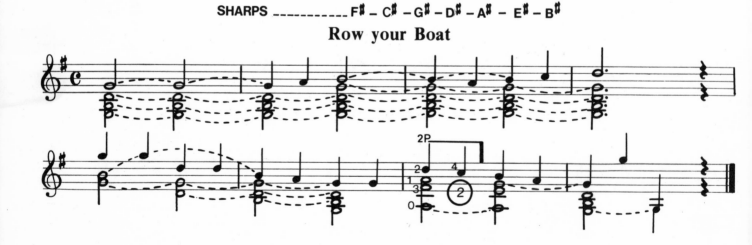

Santa Lucia

94

Intervals

An interval is the distance between one note (scale degree) and another. Intervals are usually gauged from the tonic note of that scale (keynote).

The difference between the keynote and the 4th, 5th and 8th (octave) degrees is called *perfect*. The remaining degrees (2nd, 3rd, 6th and 7th) are called *major*.

All degrees chromatically raise by one semi-tone to become *augmented*.

All major degrees chromatically lower by one semi-tone to become *minor*.

All minor and perfect degrees chromatically lower by one semi-tone to become *diminished*.

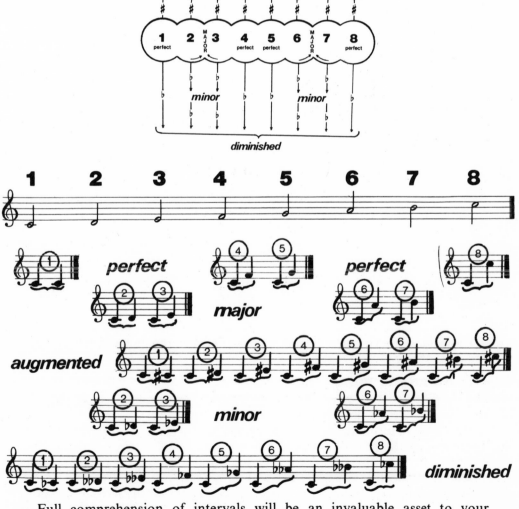

Full comprehension of intervals will be an invaluable asset to your understanding of the construction of chords.

CHAPTER 13

Minor Scale Forms

Relative minor scales

Whenever a minor scale shares the same key signature as a major scale, it is called a *relative*; the major scale becomes relative to the minor scale and vice versa.

The notation of a minor scale begins on the sub-mediant degree (6th), or minor 3rd interval below the first upper-tonic degree, of the major scale. Its construction depends on the type of minor scale it is.

The simplest of all minor scales is the 'natural' or 'pure' minor. The notation begins on the minor 3rd degree below the upper-tonic note of the major scale and then duplicates the positioning of the notes of the total scale in the allocated eight successive notes.

The A natural minor scale is relative to C major: Neither the scale of C major nor A minor has a key signature. Their tone and semi-tone areas are identical except for the tonic notes of each scale.

CONSTRUCTION FORMULA FOR THE NATURAL (PURE) MINOR

1st to 2nd degree	TONE
2nd to 3rd degree	SEMI-TONE
3rd to 4th degree	TONE
4th to 5th degree	TONE
5th to 6th degree	SEMI-TONE
6th to 7th degree	TONE
7th to 8th degree	TONE

The *natural minor* has semi-tones falling between the 2nd and 3rd, and 5th and 6th, degrees.

The harmonic minor scale

The harmonic minor scale is similar to a natural minor scale except that the 7th degree is raised one semi-tone in its construction.

The function of the harmonic minor scale differs from others in producing the basis for the adaptation of the minor key in its harmonic form. The difference between the relatives and their natural sound output resembles the difference between the major scale and its relative harmonic minor.

By means of the raised 7th degree 'harmonic note' of the harmonic minor scale one can tell whether the passage is in major or minor. The minor passage will always contain the raised 7th degree.

The notational difference between C major and A minor is that the scale of A minor contains a G sharp, whereas the relative C major has only a G natural.

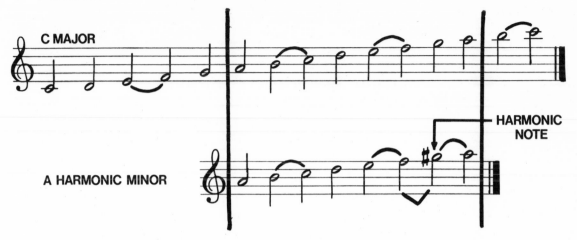

The distance between the 6th and 7th degrees of the minor scale is a tone and a half (three frets apart).

HARMONIC MINOR SCALE FORMULA

1st to 2nd degree	TONE
2nd to 3rd degree	SEMI-TONE
3rd to 4th degree	TONE
4th to 5th degree	TONE
5th to 6th degree	SEMI-TONE
6th to 7th degree	TONE AND A HALF
7th to 8th degree	SEMI-TONE

Within the harmonic minor scale the semi-tones fall between the 2nd and 3rd, 5th and 6th, and 7th and 8th degrees, with a tone and a half between the 6th and 7th degrees.

The melodic minor scale

The melodic minor scale consists of two parts: the ascending tract, where the 6th and 7th degrees are each raised by one semi-tone; and the descending tract in which they are then restored to their scale degrees (one semi-tone lower).

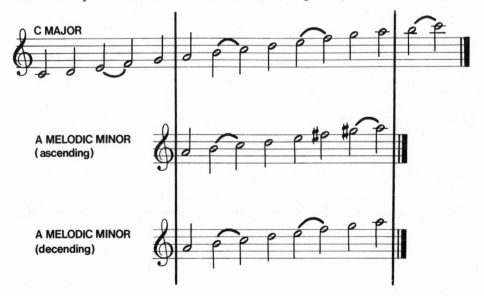

'A' Melodic Minor Scale

MELODIC MINOR SCALE FORMULA

1st to 2nd degree	TONE
2nd to 3rd degree	SEMI-TONE
3rd to 4th degree	TONE
4th to 5th degree	TONE
5th to 6th degree	TONE
6th to 7th degree	TONE
7th to 8th degree	SEMI-TONE
8th to 7th degree	TONE
7th to 6th degree	TONE
6th to 5th degree	SEMI-TONE
5th to 4th degree	TONE
4th to 3rd degree	TONE
3rd to 2nd degree	SEMI-TONE
2nd to 1st degree	TONE

The melodic minor and the harmonic minor scales are similar in containing semi-tone areas between the 2nd and 3rd, 5th and 6th, and 7th and 8th degrees. However, the melodic minor does not have the advantage of the tone and a half in its construction, and therefore has its basic impact in the production of melody rather than the construction of harmony (as the name of each scale suggests).

Despite the basic difference between the two, they are quite frequently used together.

Greensleeves

My Bonnie

CHAPTER 14

Relative Keys, Minor Key Chords and Related Construction

Minor key chords construct from the harmonic minor scale

As with the construction of the key chords from the major scale (in 3rds), the tonic, sub-dominant and dominant chords will construct from the same basic patterns.

The harmonic minor scale will, within itself, produce all the chords of the key; furthermore, the three basic chords mentioned above will appear within it.

Each chord, and its construction notes, can be arrived at by the use of 3rds, as is the case with the major scale.

TONIC CHORD	Obtain the tonic note and ascend by two 3rds. Scale degrees 1 – 3 – 5.
SUB-DOMINANT CHORD	Obtain the upper-tonic note and descend by two 3rds. Scale degrees 8 – 6 – 4.
DOMINANT CHORD	Use the internal notes of either the tonic or sub-dominant chords, and either ascend or descend by two 3rds. Scale degrees from the internal tonic, 5 – 7 – 2 – 4; or from the internal note of the sub-dominant, 4 – 2 – 7 – 5.

HARMONIC MINOR SCALE

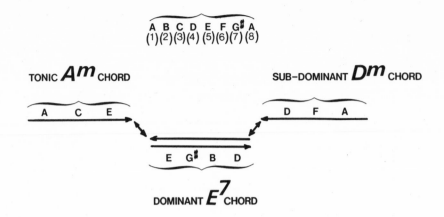

Therefore the **key of A minor** has three basic chords:

TONIC	A minor	A C E
SUB-DOMINANT	D minor	D F A
DOMINANT	E7th (seventh)	E G♯ B D

Expanding tetrachords will form keys

If two additional tetrachords are placed either side of the two tetrachords found within a scale, they will form three separate scales, which in turn combine to form a key.

Chords may also be constructed from the three independent scales by their construction formulae.

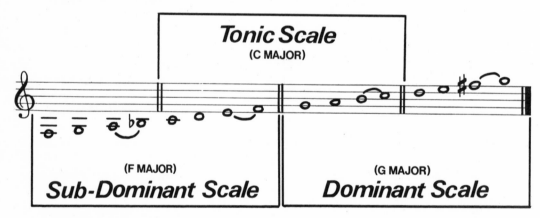

Each scale is now governed by the two tetrachords representing it. Note that although the scales overlap each other, each shares one of the tetrachords with another scale within the same key.

Each chord constructs from the relevant chord above and is applied to its formula as follows:

The principal scale is C major, and therefore no key signature is applied to any of the above chords since the key of C major has no sharps or flats.

The relative minor scale can also be formed by the same process of expanded tetrachords, although this involves the introduction of the major key of the minor 3rd interval below the original major scale—namely the scale of A minor.

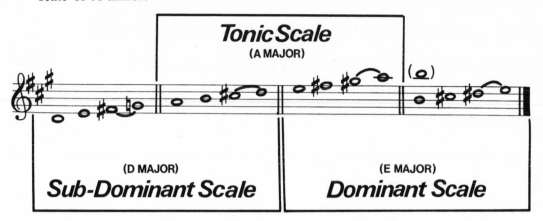

The formula of each chord will now be the minor formula, i.e. minor (♭) 3rd:

These chords have been formed from the principal chord of A major, although the (key and) chords are of the scale of A minor.

A far more suitable form would be to use the minor scale to produce chords, without further lowering the 3rd degree from the scale shown. If this were to be applied, the chords would then be written with the 1 – 3 – 5 formula, and the dominant chord would have to be formed with a formula not of its construction mode, 1 – 3 – 5 – 7.

The introduction of the harmonic minor scale would also be problematic, in as much as tetrachords could not be expanded on the present format without ruining the scale structure (since the present harmonic minor scale is T – ST – T – T – T½ – T). Therefore the only feasible solution is to apply the *dual harmonic minor scale*.

The dual harmonic minor scale

This is of unusual character, being a dual combination of the last four notes of the harmonic minor scale.

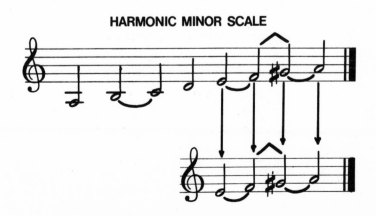

The last four notes now become an independent tetrachord formula pattern, spaced (as any other tetrachord) at one tone apart between each section of the dual harmonic minor tetrachord:

TONE APART

DUAL HARMONIC MINOR SCALE FORMULA

1st to 2nd degree	SEMI-TONE
2nd to 3rd degree	TONE AND A HALF
3rd to 4th degree	SEMI-TONE
4th to 5th degree	TONE
5th to 6th degree	SEMI-TONE
6th to 7th degree	TONE AND A HALF
7th to 8th degree	SEMI-TONE

The selection form of the dual harmonic minor scale (each being of four notes) makes this an ideal scale for expansions and extensions of the tetrachord form and nature.

The construction of minor key chords from the dual harmonic minor scale: By implementing the format of the dual harmonic minor scale, with further tetrachords (one above and another below) added to the original scale, three keys will emerge, as in the case of major scale chord extensions:

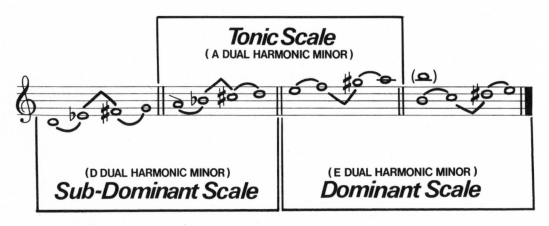

The chords concerned can still be tabulated by using the original minor formula patterns, and the minor 3rd area below can also be applied without changing the key signature of the relative minor scale.

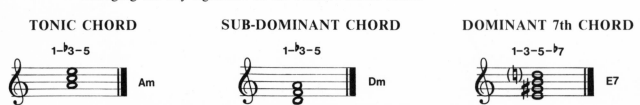

The dual harmonic minor scale, although of immense value, cannot be used for the construction of chords of the 6th extraction. Difficulty may also be experienced in the tabulation of the formulae for the 9th, etc.

You should appreciate the need (apart from its compositional value) for the dual harmonic minor scale for purposes such as the one above, and you should understand its full character as an alternate tetrachord form to the one offered by the major scale tetrachord.

Although much music is based on the form of the tetrachords, very few of these musical forms actually exist in the true tetrachord sequence.

Why scales and keys are called relative

Dictionaries define 'relative' as 'having a relation to something else'. This is the case with scales and keys.

As already proven, the relative natural minor of the same key signature as the one shared by another major has identical scale notes, although each scale commences a 3rd apart from the other.

Keys can also be proved to be relative when their subsequent tonic, sub-dominant and dominant chords are compared. Each chord will share two of its notes with its relative chord, and the remaining notes will be one tone apart.

If C major and A minor were to be taken as examples, the key of C major consists of the following chords:

TONIC	C
SUB-DOMINANT	F
DOMINANT	G7

Whereas the key of A minor consists of the following chords:

TONIC	Am
SUB-DOMINANT	Dm
DOMINANT	E7

If the above chords were to be dissected, the following observations could be made:

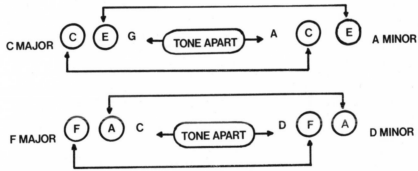

This clearly shows that in both the tonic and the sub-dominant chords there are *two constant notes*, with the remainder *one tone apart*.

The dominant 7th chords, although of four notes each, will again have two common notes. The only difference is that the remaining two notes of each of the chords are *one semi-tone apart*; therefore the two semi-tones combination will be equivalent to the area of *one tone*:

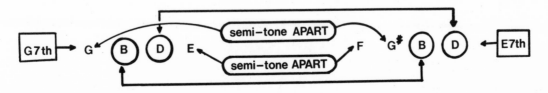

103

Jesu, Joy of Man's Desiring

PART FOUR
Added musicianship

CHAPTER 15

Unisons and
Out of Tune Guitars

Unisons

A unison can be defined as 'the duplication of any note by an instrument, or together with any other instrument, at the same pitch'.

The guitar is fortunate in this area—because of the six separate strings—and unison notes may be played, more than just once, on a lower string(s).

One example of unison tuning: By pressing behind the fifth fret of the second string, the unison of the open first string (E) can be played.

By pressing behind the ninth fret of the third string, the unison of the open first string (E) is also available.

By pressing behind the fifteenth fret of the fourth string, a further unison of the open first string (E) can also be found.

The guitar allows for up to five unison notes to be played within its immediate compass. Further unisons can also be produced by applying harmonics (see pages 115-117).

Unisons on the lower strings will be far more mellow in sound than the notes of the open, fixed or lower positions on a higher string. This is because the string length has been shortened, and the vibrations are not as acute.

Out of tune guitars

If a guitar is maintained above or below concert pitch (or out of tune at concert pitch, or with badly worn strings) for any length of time, it will gradually become affected to the point where it cannot be tuned correctly again, no matter how expert the musician tuning it may be.

Because the face of the instrument governs movement of sound, any drastic change in the harmonic production will alter the properties of the instrument to such an extent that the sound waves will no longer travel correctly at concert pitch—adjusting to the new frequency—thus limiting the vibration qualities of the instrument.

The guitar vibrates to pre-specified frequencies, improves in sound over a period of time at these frequencies, and is also pre-adjusted (during manufacture) to respond to these same frequencies. Alter the frequency pitch of the music, and this will in turn alter the frequency structure of the guitar.

Once the molecular structure of the wood has been altered (from its pre-adjusted state) it will take a very long time to return to its concert pitch response, thus rendering the instrument 'unplayable in tune at the true concert pitch' for which it was originally designed.

CHAPTER 16

Chord Construction in Brief

Chords can be simply constructed by formula from the major scale. (Detailed chord construction can be found on pages 131-138.)

Maintain constant finger notes: Whenever a lowered finger note appears constantly throughout a passage, it is far better to hold the note than to remove it.

Better finger control would be obtained by holding down the C note in the above passage.

The C note could again be maintained throughout the passage above.

Do not play music any faster than you can handle comfortably: The playing of any music must always be restricted to a speed which is comfortable for the performer—generally slower than you think you will be able to play, rather than a faster speed that will let continual mistakes occur.

First attempts at a piece should always be made with caution, for you must allow yourself time to appreciate fully the work you are about to perform in order to eliminate problems before they occur.

Correct execution of chords: Chords are sometimes written to be stopped on a lower string than the first string. To execute this, force the plectrum across the required strings, and stop on the strings just after the one written.

Stop this chord on the second string before the first string is accidentally sounded. By stopping the plectrum at the first string, only the written required notes (fifth to second strings) have been played.

CHAPTER 17   Patterns of Rhythm

Rhythmic patterns are of either *simple* or *compound time*. They are arranged in structures of *duple*, *triple* or *quadruple* form. The following areas are formulated by:

SIMPLE TIME   Undotted notation patterns
COMPOUND TIME   Dotted notation patterns

DUPLE FORM   Two distinct accents per bar
TRIPLE FORM   Three distinct accents per bar
QUADRUPLE FORM   Four distinct accents per bar

In simple time patterns, the bar accent will fall on the first bar beat of each style used:

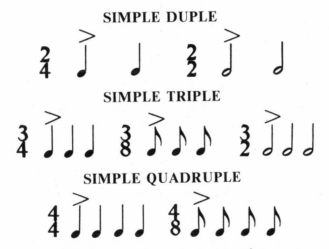

However, the compound time pattern allows for a ✳ secondary accent to be applied within its structure:

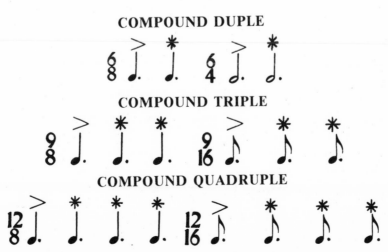

Because of this secondary accent, all music written in the compound time style must be written with an imaginary line (bar) in each of the secondary accent areas:

Unlike the simple time style, compound time cannot be abused in its set pattern. The compound time formula of accents always governs the duration of each note. If this duration is to be extended beyond its allowable dotted note margin, it must be lengthened by a tie sign within the bar concerned.

The following example is incorrect in the first writing, whereas the second example has been corrected as compound time:

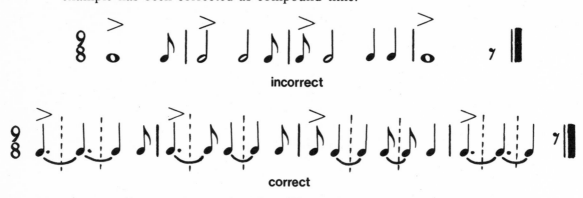

Accentation may be required for different forms. Music may be written in either compound time or simple time depending on how the accentation is placed:

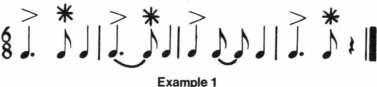

Or it may be written in simple time as:

Note that the simple time example does not adhere strictly to the rule that the structure must be of three equal sections of undotted notation within the bar, whereas the identical pattern in compound time does adhere to the required pattern of compound duple (two equal areas of dotted notation per bar).

CHAPTER 18

Position Playing

Position playing simply means that the whole hand moves along the fingerboard to the desired notational area.

Notation that begins on, say, the seventh position now commands the left-hand index finger to play on the notes of the seventh fret:

1st finger	–	seventh fret
2nd finger	–	eighth fret
3rd finger	–	ninth fret
4th finger	–	tenth fret
4th finger	–	eleventh fret

The left-hand thumb must also move, and be placed directly behind the centre of the new position of the fingers in use. It is not enough to place the left-hand thumb in any position just near the fingers being applied in position.

Do not overplay any selected passage of music: You should always try to sight-read any passage of music. While prolonged study of any passage will enable you to memorise it, there is the possibility that mistakes made (in the writing, or in your studying) will also be memorised.

Always try to vary the amount of music you play each day. Do not be concerned about what others may think if you decide to add selected music studies to your constantly changing repertoire. The greater the scope of music attempted, the greater the possibility of obtaining an extremely accurate understanding of music through sight-reading.

Problems may of course occur if you attempt music of a standard far in excess of your capabilities. This will only tend to stagnate and frustrate your progress, and proficiency of performance will only be achieved after a great deal of memorisation has taken place.

The Can Can

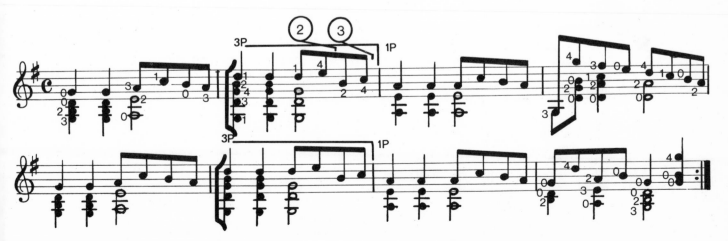

Joshua Fit the Battle of Jericho

Amazing Grace

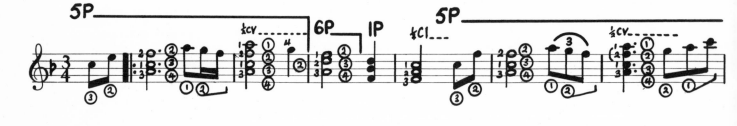

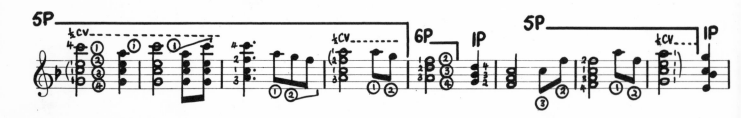

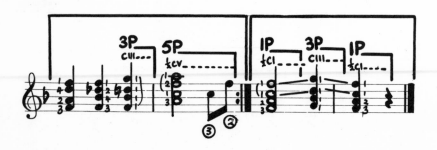

He's Got the Whole World in His Hands

John Brown's Body

The House of the Rising Sun

Blow the Man Down

Beautiful Dreamer

Blue Tail Fly

114

CHAPTER 19

Natural Harmonics— Their Construction and Effects

A harmonic is a falsetto note produced by placing the fleshy tip of the finger over the fret while taking care that the finger does not stop the string on the fret.

Each string will produce a dominant 7th chord through its harmonics. The tonic note of each dominant 7th chord is the string note.

Each harmonic note is shown at concert pitch. If these notes were to be reproduced on the guitar they naturally would have to be played one octave higher, which is the reason for the 8ve (octave) sign.

The vibrating strings will produce harmonics within themselves, and the resonance of each string is far greater at a lower pitch than at a higher pitch. For this reason the following explanations have been based on the sixth string.

If string of the same width were used, it would rise in pitch in proportion to the length by which it is shortened. The string would also rise in pitch if tension were identical and a thinner string were used. Therefore sound relies on tension and width.

Furthermore, the pitch properties would not only raise the string pitch but would also construct in scale 3rds if the vibrations were stopped at any one given length (harmonic).

Resonating notes at their exact half and quarter lengths would reproduce the (harmonic) notes higher by octaves.

Harmonics at the twelfth fret, midway in the total string length, would produce a harmonic one octave higher than the original note:

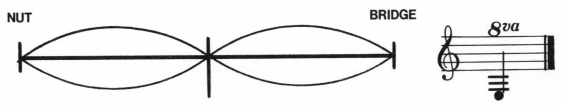

TWELFTH FRET HARMONIC

Stopping the string at a quarter of its length would also reproduce the string tonic note, but at an octave higher than the twelfth fret harmonic and two octaves higher than the original string pitch:

FIFTH FRET HARMONIC

If the string is stopped at one third of its length it will produce the tonic scale 5th of that string, again one octave higher:

SEVENTH FRET HARMONIC

Stopping the string at the middle of its one-third distance (one sixth) will reproduce the scale 5th again, two octaves higher than the scale degree and one octave higher than the seventh fret 5th degree:

3⅓ FRET HARMONIC

If the string is stopped at one fifth of its total distance it will reproduce the tonic scale 3rd degree (at two separate points) two octaves above the scale 3rd degree. The reason for the two separate points being two octaves above the 3rd scale degree is that the sound will take effect in much the same manner as if the string were stopped in quarters. Two separate areas are involved prior to the twelfth fret and each is an identical distance from the other, and therefore each will resonate at the higher pitch level:

FOURTH/NINTH FRET HARMONIC

Stopping the string at one seventh its distance will add one additional scale 3rd above the scale 5th degree. In the construction of extended chords, the dominant 7th chord 7th degree is of (minor 7th) ♭7th extraction from the major scale concerned. The note fortunately is the required extension ♭7th at a harmonic ratio two octaves higher than the original string pitch scale degree:

2⅔ FRET HARMONIC

HARMONICS AS CONSTRUCTED ON EACH OF
THE SIX STRINGS

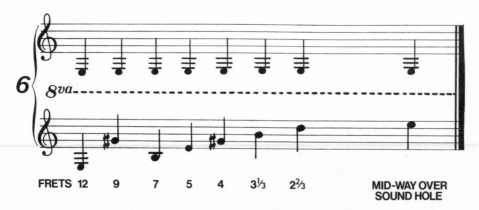

CHAPTER 20

The Benefits of a Wider Musical Knowledge

Any musician who imagines that all there is to music is his own instrument is a fool.

Music is universal, and is shared by dozens of instruments. Every musician should know something about the different types and styles of instruments; about how they constrast or blend with one another; and about how his own instrument compares with others.

For centuries musicians have been transcribing solo passages from other instruments in order to increase their available repertoires. In addition, so as not to lose the original quality in the course of transcription, many pieces have been orchestrated with acute changes of instrumental blending in the process.

Because each instrument will have pitch or mechanical properties similar to those of another instrument, it is suggested that you first study and compare the properties of the most common related instruments. After your introduction to alternate instrumentation, select the instrument you most easily recognise, taking care that it is of a type that is relevant to your own style of approach to instrumentation.

You should not restrict your knowledge of music to one clef; nor should your knowledge be restricted to only one form of transposition. As the properties of the instruments change, so too will the musical concepts of their performance characteristics.

Remember, there is more than just one musical instrument in use today.

More musical terms

Ad libitum   at pleasure, quite   freely
Agitato   with agitation
Allargando   becoming broader
Allegretto   moderately fast
Animato   with animation
Assai   very
Attacca   go on at once
Ben marcato   well marked
Calando   getting softer and slower
Cantabile   in a singing style
Cantando   in a singing style
Con anima   with feeling
Con brio   with spirit
Con forza   with force
Con grazia   with grace
Con moto   with movement
Da capo al fine   from the   beginning to the word *'fine'*
Dal segno   from the sign
Dolce   soft and sweet
Dolente   sadly, plaintively
Doloroso   sadly, plaintively
Forte piano (fp)   loud then   immediately soft
Giocoso   gay, merry
Grave   slow and solemn
Grazioso   gracefully
Largamente   broadly
Larghetto   rather broadly

Largo broadly
Leggiero lightly
Lento slowly
L'istesso tempo at the same speed
Loco at normal pitch (after 8va sign)
Main droite (M.D.) right hand
Main gauche (M.G.) left hand
Maestoso majestic
Meno mosso slower
Mezzo forte (mf) moderately loud
Mezzo piano (mp) moderately soft
Mezzo staccato moderately short and detached
Molto very
Morendo dying away
Non troppo not too much
Opus a work or a group of works
Perdendosi fading away
Pesante heavily
Piacevole pleasant, agreeable
Piu mosso quicker
Poco a little
Portamento a smooth gliding
from one note to another (as in
singing or string playing)
Prestissimo extremely fast, or as
fast as possible
Quasi as if, as it were
Rinforzando reinforcing the tone
Risoluto with resolution
Rubato with some freedom in the time
Scherzando playfully
Sempre always
Senza without
Sforzando (sf) a strong accent
Smorzando dying away
Sostenuto sustained
Sotto voce softly, in an undertone
Stringendo pressing on faster
Subito suddenly
Tempo comodo at a comfortable speed
Tempo giusto at a consistent speed
Tenuto held
Tranquillo calmly
Tre corde release the soft pedal
Una corda with the soft pedal
Vivace lively, spirited
Vivo lively, spirited

PART FIVE

Graded scales and arpeggios

CHAPTER 21

Scales and Arpeggios

The practice of scales and their relevant arpeggios should never be approached as a chore, or as one of the punishments of learning music.

The scale, within itself, is the basis of all music writing, composition and harmony. Practice should be approached with an appreciation of the knowledge to be gained through continual repetition of a serialised formula, namely the scale. Furthermore, fingering will improve (together with technique) while the scale is being studied, for its proper study will without doubt encompass the range of the guitar neck.

The arpeggio, as previously stated, is a series of notes, which are the individual notes of the tonic, sub-dominant and dominant chords of the scale concerned.

All of the following scales and arpeggios are of a systematic form. Each page contains not only the major scale but also its relative minor scale in both the harmonic and melodic forms. To these are added the relevant scale arpeggios in both major and minor.

Memorising can be made easier by the use of numbers for similarly patterned scales. Note that *the similarity in patterns is related to (and not the same as) that of another scale.* Although the fingering has been made easier by the use of systems, each note of each of the individual scales must be learnt independently.

The same approach must be used in the study of the scale arpeggio. However, instead of the number system used with the scales, the arpeggios have been shown in alphabetical forms.

It will also be found that there is duplication in the arpeggio patterns. This will happen naturally, since each scale will overlap another area of scale through its tetrachord form. The tonic chord of C major will remain C major, whereas the C major chord will be the sub-dominant chord of the G major scale.

Care should be taken at all times in the study of the scale and its relevant arpeggios. They should, if possible, be studied daily, and each note of each scale and each arpeggio should be thoroughly known before you move on to the following area.

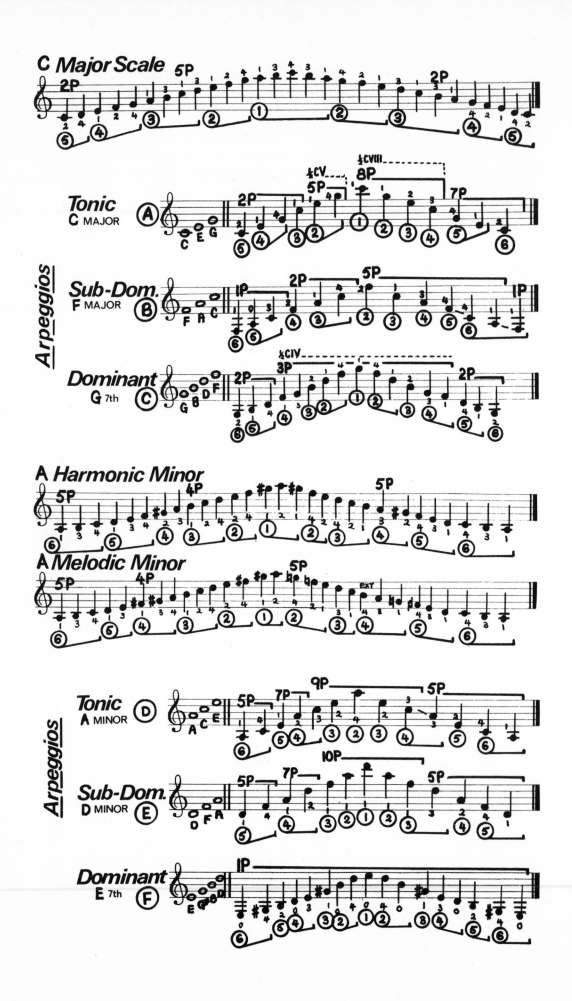

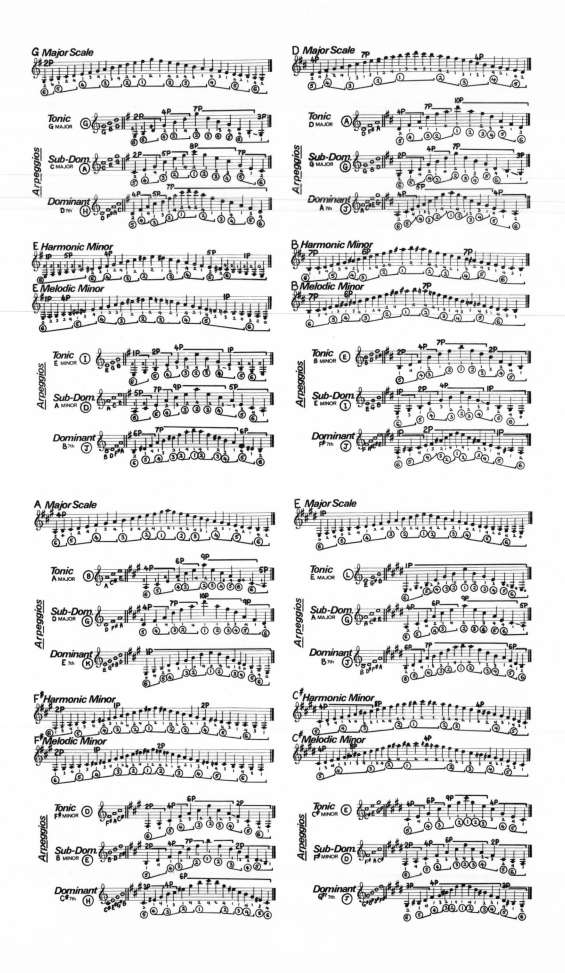

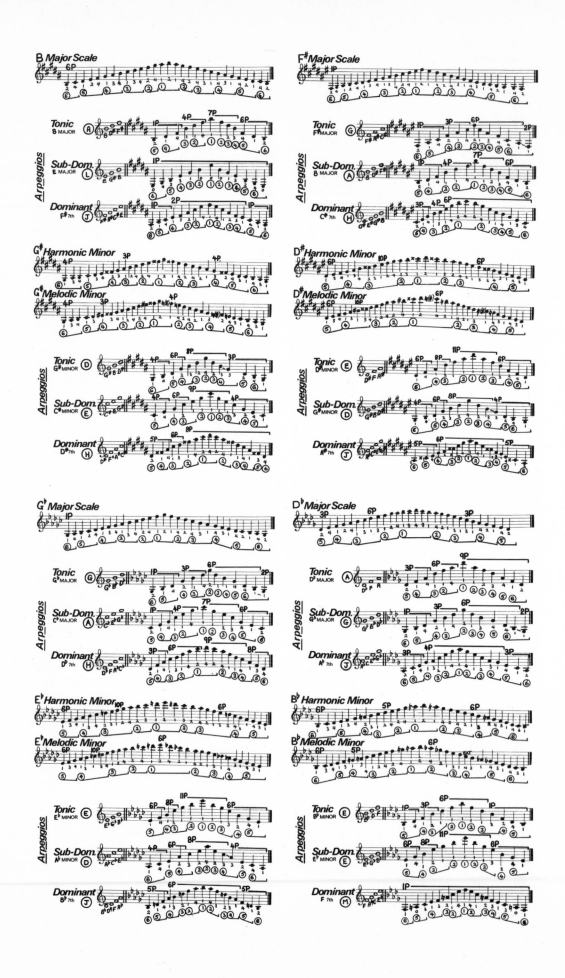

124

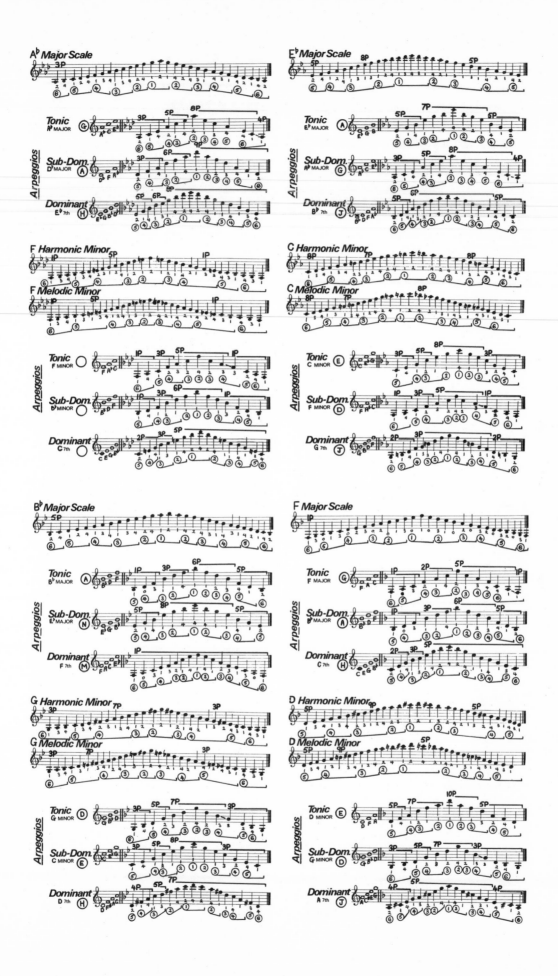

CHAPTER 22   Other Musical Scales

Scales are not fixed in terms of major or minor. In fact, the scale form is only a formal explanation (analysis) of the way that music is to be expressed, or the rule that the music must adhere to in its construction.

Western music has tended to categorise itself within a limited scope regarding the nature of the scale; consequently we are obliged to understand fully only the scales of the chromatic, major and minor forms.

Many teachers (and musicians) tend to forget that the mode, a derivative of the scale, was used in early church music. The majority of modes were in use until about the end of the sixteenth century, after which they gradually began to fall into obscurity.

Modern revision and analysis of medieval folk forms and chordal works has in recent years prompted the reintroduction and re-usage of these scales and modes. The modern composer (always searching for a more up to date approach to the contemporary sound he is prepared to experiment with) has also helped to rekindle interest in the alternate scales and modes. Various ethnic scales from Central Europe, and many others from the music of the cultures of the East, have been reintroduced. It is now becoming a must, rather than just an added study, to understand and apply such scales and modes to music in the present era.

The following scales have been set out alphabetically by their individual names, and (arbitrarily) have been written from the commencement note of C. This is applied for consistency with the style of this book, although the scales or modes may commence on any note within the enharmonic (or chromatic) range of music. The scales are also written in their note to note range. The formation of their tonal sequence (tone, semi-tone, etc.) is left to you for the final analysis of whatever form you may choose.

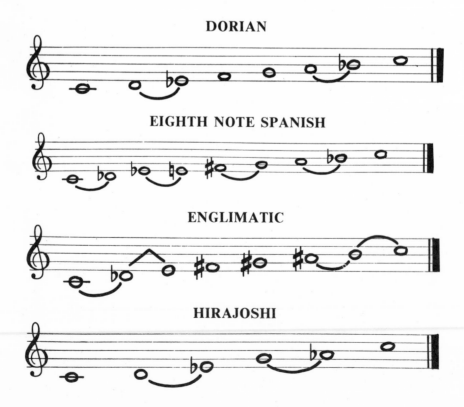

DORIAN

EIGHTH NOTE SPANISH

ENGLIMATIC

HIRAJOSHI

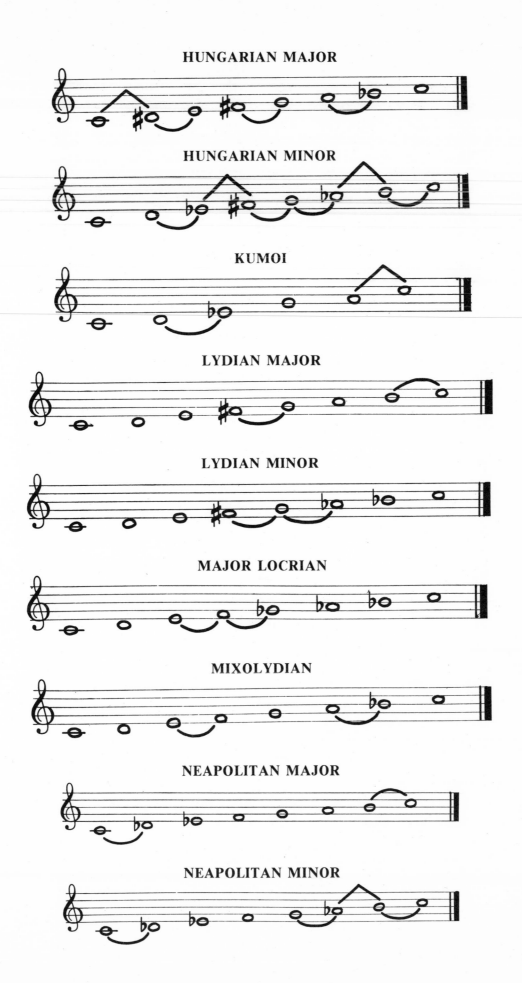

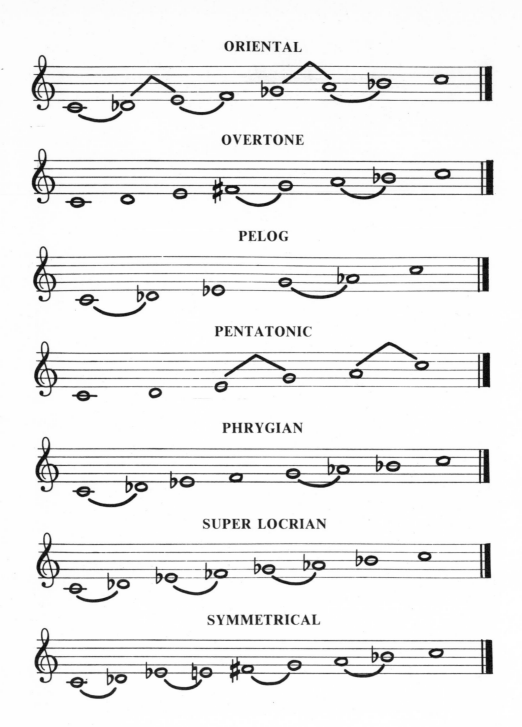

PART SIX

Advanced chords, harmonisation and extensions

CHAPTER 23
Chords—
Their Purpose and Application

Chords play a fascinating role in the structure and harmonisation of music. When dissected into their independent notes they can facilitate composition, or permit new chords and harmonies to be built on their individual notes. Whichever way a chord is applied, it cannot work without the aid of scale forms—either for its construction, or for the method of producing melodious structures and harmonies.

Scales can also be written in the form of chords, where the fundamental purpose of the chord is to complement and harmonise music. When applied to chords, scales will also form the basis for composition and arrangement.

Categorically, chords are simple. Each note depends on a successive interval to fix its position in the harmonisation of the other notes around it. The chord expands within itself. The added notes of the chord do not change its function or purpose, but tend to realise a richer, fuller meaning and sound characteristic.

Modern music has let the 'full bodied' harmonic balance of the chord show through areas of composition in the fields of jazz, Latin American, modern blues, etc., and other contemporary music. Even with these new styles, the properties and methods of combinations are not new. They are simply played against an enriched rhythmic pattern of chords and their individual note structure.

The melody must at all times be prevalent. Irrespective of how the chords are applied, their main purpose is to add colour to the harmonisation of the melody in hand. Instruments will blend together and, between them, work to a harmonisation of chordal patterns or even work experimentally away from each other; either further colouring or distorting the structure of the melody as they combine in, and with, the chords.

The style of the modern harmonies and chordal extensions is not new—it has now been with us for some 300 years. It is interesting to note that harmony acceptable to the ear has been developed exclusively by the European races. It has changed dramatically in different periods, but its basic concept has remained unaltered during these three centuries. This period takes in many enlightening developments, and is one which includes a multitude of varieties and styles from such notable composers as Bach, Schubert, Wagner, Handel, Mozart, Mendelssohn, Haydn, Corelli, Schumann, Purcell, Beethoven, Berlioz, Liszt and Chopin; and also from such forerunners of guitar styles as Sor, De Visée, Purcell, Carulli, Schumann, Tarrega, Carcassi, Diabelli, Albeniz, Giuliani, Paganini, Aguado and Milan.

No matter what individual styles, motives and experiments contributed to the music of these composers, the structure of their chords was the same as chord structure today.

A brief look at the main musical periods in the past three centuries shows a great deal of variety of composition.

The first of these periods could be best described as J. S. Bach's era: the **Baroque Period** (seventeenth to eighteenth centuries), which can be looked upon as a time of technically luxuriant decoration. Even today it can be said that 'if you can play Bach, you can play music', for his compositions and inventions are among the most difficult and detailed available. He rarely harmonised in the traditional sense, but involved harmonies of up to eleven lines of music together at the one time.

The **Classic Period** (eighteenth to early nineteenth centuries) was based on simplicity of style: melody with the simplest of harmonies. The basic aim was to achieve perfection in the 'beauty of simplicity'. It was also the period that gave birth to chamber music and to Mozart, its most significant composer.

The **Romantic Period** (early to late nineteenth century) was one of research, new instruments and new techniques. It was during this period that the guitar emerged as an instrument in its own right—and was at last composed for exclusively—rather than as a tool of transcription. The guitar was given its sixth string (E), two octaves below its first string, thus enhancing its range; and the birth of the concert classical guitar saw an enlarged body (in width and depth), which resulted in an instrument of far better balance and volume. The Romantic Period emphasised the expression of emotion, and sometimes its music has too sentimental an aura. But the harmonies are exacting, and can be heard at their finest in the works of such composers as Chopin, Beethoven, Brahms, Mendelssohn and Strauss. The guitar also had outstanding composers in Sor, Aguado, Carcassi and Carulli.

Although each of these composers has an individual style of composition, overall harmonies tend to sound much the same. The major exception is Sor, whose works differ greatly from the others, for he relied a great deal on technicalities in performance. Another notable composing at the end of this period was Tarrega, whose beautiful and technically difficult works earned him the title 'the Chopin of the guitar'.

The harmony style attributed to the Romantic Period is still being applied at present. But there are also the nonconformist (or non-traditional) composers who write in a totally 'ad lib' disharmonised style. While the basis of harmonies remains constant, new and enlightening (throbbing) rhythmns require a better technical understanding of chords and of their relevant combinations and structures. It is for this reason that a comprehensive knowledge of the extensions of chords will be an invaluable asset to the modern pupil.

CHAPTER 24 Construction, Abbreviations, and Major, Minor and Dominant Chords

Rules of construction
All chordal constructions are based on a progressive system of 3rds from a major scale:

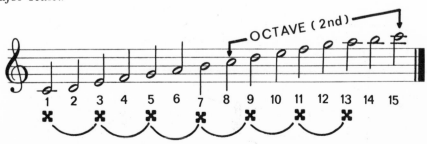

If the influence of the interval structures that govern the nature of each individual chord can be understood, the categories of chords can be described as:

Any chord containing the perfect 5th degree
is called a *common chord*.

Of the available common chords there are four basic principles to realise:

Any chord with a major 3rd is called a *major*.
Any chord with a minor 3rd is called a *minor*.
Any chord with an augmented 5th is called *augmented*.

The pattern should follow in such a way that the chord containing the diminished 5th degree should be called *diminished*, whereas it may be of a flattened 5th or a diminished chord form depending on the structure of its interval of the 3rd degree (refer to the section on diminished chords, pages 137).

All chords must originate on the keynote and must be constructed in their root position. Inversions of chords can be applied at any time after the initial common chord construction. It is the basic formula that constructs a chord, whereas its inversion may in turn construct another chord.

Major chords

The major chord is simply a construction of 3rds in the form 1 – 3 – 5:

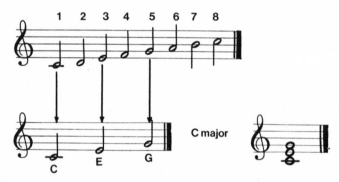

It is a common chord due to its major 5th, and is called major because the 3rd degree is an interval of the major form.

Intervals between notes follow a pattern of 1 – 3 (major 3rd) to 3 – 5 (minor 3rd), whereby the 3rd degree is the influencing factor of the chord; the 5th, being the perfect 5th, is simply a major.

If two or more intervals are written in a cluster of notes, they are of *enharmonic extraction*. As the notes separate into arpeggios they become known as *melodic*, and each can be separately harmonised as a separate chord for each of the notes concerned.

Minor chords

The minor chord is also a common chord, with perfect 5th and minor 3rd intervals:

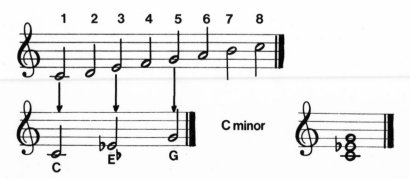

Its construction is that of 3rds (1 – 3 – 5), lowering its 3rd degree (major) one semi-tone lower to minor and consequently creating the formula 1 – ♭3 – 5.

Progressive intervals are of interest, for they are the reverse of the major: 1 – b♭ (minor 3rd) – 5 (major 3rd). Because the 3rd degree is minor, and the 5th is perfect, the chord is known as minor.

**'SEMI-TONE'
CHANGE of THIRDS**

All extensions of 3rds will show the form of either the major or the minor chord, since only a change in the 3rd degree will alter their name.

Dominant 7th chord

The dominant 7th is the most frequently used and influential chord in music. It is a chord that blends perfectly in any major or minor key, and has constant properties of each scale note of that key in a dominating effect.

If the 3rd degree is extended above the common chord, and the 7th degree lowered to a minor 7th, the dominant 7th chord will emerge:

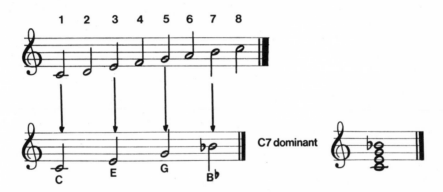

Although the minor 7th note is used, the dominant 7th chord cannot be called minor. It has already been established that the minor chord can only be called minor if the 3rd degree is of minor form—the dominant 7th chord has its 3rd degree in major.

The chord also establishes itself within a scale. It extracts its four notes without showing its ♭7th extraction, for it is utilised within the scale of the perfect 5th below itself (inverted perfect 4th) and applies to the extracted scale degrees of 5 – 7 – 2 – 4 (2 – 4 – 5 – 7).

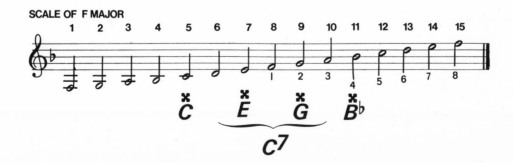

The dominant 7th is also the most important chord within the scope of modern harmony. Its interval progression is interesting: major 3rd, perfect 5th, minor 7th—encompassing one of each of the minimal intervals.

Minor 7th chord: Lower the 3rd degree of the dominant 7th chord.

Major 7th chord: Restore the ♭7th degree to the scale major interval (7th).

DOMINANT 7th	MINOR 7th	MAJOR 7th
MAJOR 3rd	MINOR 3rd	MAJOR 3rd
PERFECT 5th	PERFECT 5th	PERFECT 5th
MINOR 7th	MINOR 7th	MAJOR 7th

All chords of the 7th, and extensions of the 7th, are called *fundamental discords*.

Abbreviations of chords: Due to the methods you may study, or books you may read or play from, you could become rather confused by the terminology applied to the abbreviated chord symbols. The method used primarily is of English extraction but, because of the vast number of publications of the American system, the two methods have been incorporated here (wherever possible) to facilitate understanding of the two systems.

Two modes of explanation are applied here and throughout the remainder of this book in terms of the construction of chords. Unfortunately the tables will become quite large, and it is important that each of the names be thoroughly understood since they can fluctuate greatly in the American system where the composer or arranger has a free hand in the naming of chords.

The chord as universally accepted is written first, and its additive variations are placed in brackets:

MAJOR	(without symbol)	(CM, no variants)
MINOR	Cm	(C mi, C−, C−3, C♭3)
7th	C7	(C (♭7), C−7m, Cx)
MINOR 7th	Cm7	(C mi 7)
MAJOR 7th	C maj 7	(CM7, C−Large, CL, C Alt)

The word dominant 7th is commonly only used to describe the chord, and is not included in the symbol which is simply shown as 7.

CHAPTER 25

Augmented Chords and Whole Tone Application

Augmented C⁺ (C aug, C aug5, C♯5, C⁺5)

The augmented is an extremely significant chord in the construction of harmonies, etc. Unfortunately it is seldom (or too briefly) explained in guitar tutors. Many guitarists are quite afraid of the augmented chord, despite its significance.

Its construction is that of a common chord with an augmented 5th (♯5) degree:

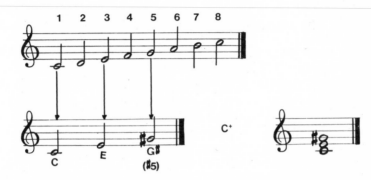

Intervals are of interest since they construct in major 3rd to augmented 5th in a sequence of major 4rd to major 3rd. Therefore if enharmonics are applied there will be only four augmented chords:

The complete chromatic range of augmented chords can be tabled from the chords shown above.

Whole tone scale

The whole tone scale is a scale consisting entirely of tones. Because of this structure the whole tone scale is a scale of six consecutive tones (seven if the upper-tonic note is included, always written enharmonically as the keynote). The scale can only be of two pitches, C or C♯(D♭), and may commence on any given note within the chromatic range since there are no semi-tones to define its position. It is also of interest that chords cannot be built from the scale degrees.

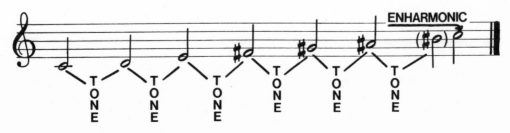

If the scale were written in triads of its 1st, 3rd and 5th degrees, a new scale of augmented chords (one tone apart) would emerge:

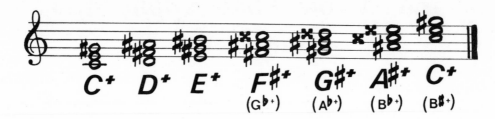

The whole tone harmonisation of the augmented chords is used purely to describe the positions of the chords moving in interval proportions of two consecutive major 3rd intervals, and subsequently why it allows for only four total enharmonically adjusted areas of augmented chords. You should however be aware of the colouring potential of the augmented chord applied to the harmonisation of music.

Augmented 7th chords   C⁺7 (C7⁺, C7 aug 5, C7♯5, C7⁺5)

A dominant 7th chord with the augmented 5th degree (1 – 3 –♯5 – ♭7).

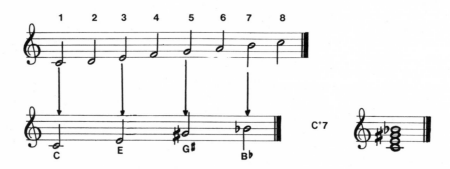

More common than imagined, the dominant must be appreciated as a chord of great influence, and the raised 5th degree should not be seen as an unusual colouring of harmonies.

The interval structure is: major 3rd, augmented 5th, minor 7th.

1 – 3 (major 3rd) 3 – ♯5 (major 3rd) ♯5 – ♭7 (diminished 3rd)

Notice the diminished 3rd at the end of the chord (refer to the chapter on diminished chords) and the tone and a half or minor 3rd structure.

Augmented minor 7th chord Cm⁺7 (Cm7 aug 5, Cm7⁺, Cm7 5, Cm7♯5, C mi7⁺5)

Constructed as the augmented 7th but with a minor 3rd degree (1 – ♭3 – ♯5 – ♭7).

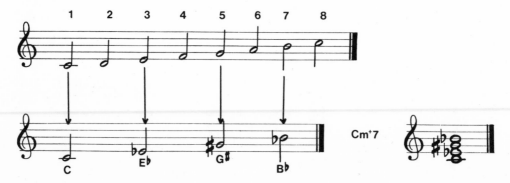

CHAPTER 26

Diminished Chords and Continuing Minor 3rd Application

Diminished chords   C° (C dim)

A minor chord with the diminished 5th interval (1 – ♭3 – ♭5).

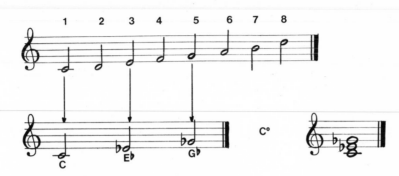

The diminished chord is based on the minor 3rd to diminished 5th, or the movement of two diminished 3rd degrees.

Modern music does not fully accept this form of diminished chord (although allowable in some construction) but involves the approach of the further minor 3rd degree to the ♭♭7 interval, being the *diminished 7th chord.*

The diminished 7th chord C° or C° 7 (C dim, C dim7, C7°, C-7): The diminished 7th chord is an expansion of the diminished chord by one additional minor 3rd degree to the scale construction formula of 1 – ♭3 – ♭5 –♭ ♭7:

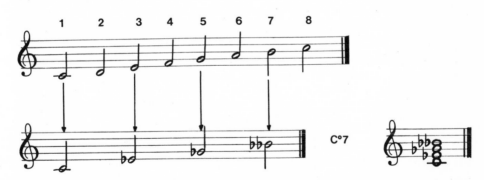

The construction of this chord is 1 – ♭3 (minor 3rd), ♭3 – ♭5 (diminished 5th), ♭5 – ♭ ♭7 (diminished 7th). The interval steps are minor 3rds. If another minor 3rd degree were included in the construction it would return (enharmonically) to the upper-tonic note, thus being the only perfectly constructed repetitious chord in music.

At times the chord is written as 1 – ♭3 – ♭5 – 6, the 6th being enharmonic to the ♭ ♭7th. **This is incorrect.**

The 6th degree allows for correct enharmonic interval placement, but names quite differently from the interval positioning of the scale (major 6th). Consequently, all thoughts of construction by enharmonic intervals should be forgotten.

If enharmonics are to be employed, why then is the ♭5th (diminished 5th) interval not placed enharmonically as a ♯4th, as is the enharmonic 6th? The structure constructed enharmonically would then be disjointed 1 – b3 – ♯4 – 6, and would mean absolutely nothing to the musician since the 5th degree is omitted.

Why then apply a 6th as the enharmonic to the ♭♭7th?

The chord is called diminished and must be written with this idea in mind. All constructions must accordingly follow ♭♭7th (diminished 7th).

There are only three diminished 7th chords: Intervals of the diminished 7th chords fall one and a half tones apart and therefore allow for two further diminished chords to be written between the principal diminished chord:

$$C - C\sharp (D\flat) - D \text{ only}$$

All other construction can be formulated enharmonically.

Enharmonic placement plays a great part in the tabulation and the naming of the diminished chords.

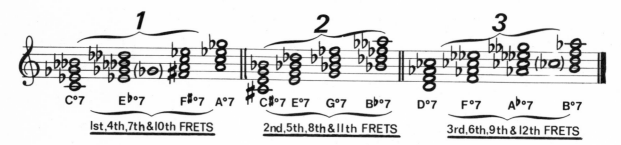

An understanding of the prospects of the diminished 7th chord is essential for all musicians. Guitarists tend to have an inbuilt fear of the diminished chord, mainly due to their lack of understanding of its harmonic value or the progression of its construction.

The diminished chord, once applied, will reproduce itself (with the same fingering) three frets ascending from the position played continually.

The diminished 7th chord is usually acceptably termed the diminished chord, and is at most times just called the diminished. It is not hard to understand why, for the diminished 7th is only a minor 3rd (equal interval) above the diminished triad. American music also tends to confuse the terminology and use of the chord, thereby complicating its simplicity.

138

CHAPTER 27

Major and Minor Scale Harmonisation

Major scale in triads

If the major scale is written from its tonic, mediant and dominant notes (in clusters of triads) the basis of harmony will construct.

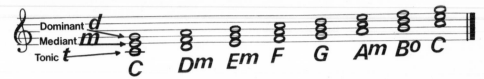

The chords formed are of major and minor extraction, whereas the 7th degree is diminished (or can be expanded to become the diminished 7th chord). This progression is one of the basic formulae of music composition that has become commercially popular in the past ten years.

It is interesting to note that the scale of triads (major) within itself contains the key chords of C major and also the key chords of its relative minor, A minor. The odd chord is the 7th degree chord of diminished form.

This pattern of chords cannot be abused. In whatever sequence they are placed, they will always sound correct. Whatever the melody line, one of the chords of the major scale of triads will blend (if the music is in a major key), irrespective of the placement of the melody note and irrespective of the inversion in which the chord is placed.

The simplicity of this scale also lends itself to extensions of the chords being applied.

Harmonic minor scale in triads

Written in triads like the major scale of triads, but commencing on its relative harmonic minor note (chord).

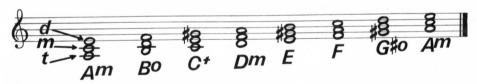

Certain common factors are easily seen in the two scales of triads:

> In each, these chords remain unchanged—
> Am, B°, Dm, F
>
> The C chord becomes a C$^+$ chord.
>
> The Em chord becomes an E chord.
>
> The G chord becomes the G$^{\sharp}$° chord, the new harmonic note chord that is the harmonic note chord of the minor scale.

Because each scale closely resembles the other in the majority of chords, and two chords are coloured differently (realising that the 7th degree is the leading note chord), it now allows for modulation between the two keys to become more of a reality than a possibility.

As with the major scale of triads it does not matter how this particular scale of triads is applied. It is the second most widely used basis for composition in present-day music.

The following table shows the structure of each scale triad in a more enlightening way:

'CHORD'	Major SCALE	Harmonic Minor SCALE
Major	1 - 4 - 5	5 - 6
Minor	2 - 3 - 6	1 - 4
Augmented	-	3
Diminished	7	2 - 7

At a quick glance, the harmonic minor scale appears to have a better balance of chords. This is only in appearance, and each scale has one basic influencing chord: the 7th (diminished chord) in the major; and the 3rd (augmented chord) in the harmonic minor.

It is important to note that the major scale has a better chordal distribution than the harmonic minor scale.

CHAPTER 28

Chordal Analysis

Review of the basic 7th chords

The 7th chord plays an extremely important role in music, and is also the basis of extensions within chords.

Analyse each chord carefully, for each will play an important role in the applications and extensions of the notational forms within chords.

DOMINANT 7th	MAJOR 7th	MINOR 7th	DIMINISHED 7th	AUGMENTED 7th
♭7	7	♭7	♭♭7	♭7
5	5	5	♭5	♯5
3	3	♭3	♭3	3
1	1	1	1	1

B♭	B	B♭	B♭♭	B♭
G	G	G	G♭	G♯
E	E	E♭	E♭	E
C	C	C	C	C

To this nucleus, the extension of chords can be added at the writer's pleasure. All further extensions of chords will be written only in the major form or, if further explanation of style is warranted, other variations of minor, etc., will be added. Therefore it is up to the student to implement the above structures in the additional chord formations.

CHAPTER 29

Advanced Intervals and Extension of Chordal Patterns

Compound intervals

The compound interval is the interval found above the compass of the eight note diatonic scale:

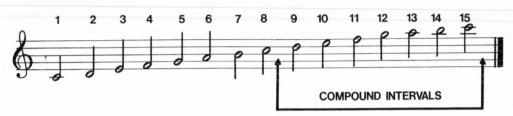

In the compound form the intervals are:

PERFECT 11 – 12– 15
MAJOR   9 – 10 – 13 – 14

The raising and lowering of the intervals is of the same structure as that found within the first octave—major and perfect rise to augmented, etc. Comprehension of these intervals will be of value in the construction of extended chords (9th, etc.).

Inverted intervals

If an interval, such as a perfect 5th (C – G), is inverted, the latter note becomes the keynote and the interval converts to a perfect 4th (G – C).

PERFECT	intervals will remain	PERFECT
MAJOR	intervals will invert to	MINOR
MINOR	intervals will invert to	MAJOR
DIMINISHED	intervals will invert to	AUGMENTED
AUGMENTED	intervals will invert to	DIMINISHED

It is interesting to note that all inversions will be in multiples of nine:

MAJOR 2nd	inverts to	MINOR 7th	(9)
PERFECT 4th	inverts to	PERFECT 5th	(9), etc.

The inversion to patterns of nine is due to the conversion of the keynote. The 2nd note of any scale will invert to the 7th note if reversed, and so on.

Chords extending on the dominant 7th chords

Further extensions of chords beyond the dominant 7th position are chords that contain the dominant 7th chord inclusive of the ratio of additional construction in 3rds.

All extended chords are named with the dominant 7th being predominant in all positions, and the extension is placed in brackets immediately after the dominant chord:

C7 (9)
C7 (add 9)
C7 (11)
C7 (♭11)
C7 (13), etc.

There are many other names for each of the chords being extended; these can be found at the end of each section of extensions.

Extended triads form additional chords within

Any chord that expands beyond the standard triad (major, minor, augmented or diminished) by a ratio of 3rds will form further chords within itself.

The example below shows the construction of the C7th chord (a chord consisting of one additional note above the standard triad). A chord commencing on its 3rd degree will construct as an additional chord, E°.

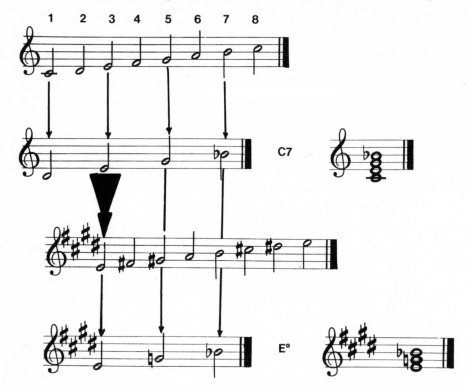

It should be noted that the 3rd degree is of the C major scale form; and if a chord were to be constructed from it, it should therefore relate to the scale note being the 1st degree of the new chord.

Because the 3rd degree of C major is an E, the new scale should therefore be E major.

By the degree relation to the new chord within the E major scale, it is found that both the 3rd and 5th degrees have each been shown one semi-tone higher. Therefore, by applying the chord formula 1 – ♭3 – ♭5 there is no question that the chord commencing on the 3rd degree is of the diminished form.

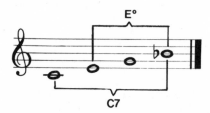

It is now feasible to conclude that the C7th chord is a combination of two separate chords. The first is C major (commencing on the mediant note of the original scale:

Further analysis will show that the two chords are a combination of both the tonic and leading note chords of the scale of F major in the 'scale of triads' formation; as the C7th chord is the dominant chord of the F major scale:

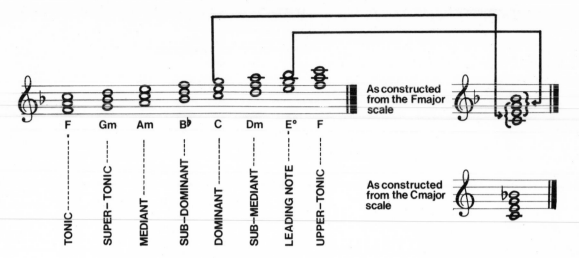

It is already understood that the dominant 7th chord of any key is of four note capacity. The above explanation thus adds strength to the dominating quality of the key dominant chord.

By comparison the C minor 7th (Cm7) chord is again of two separate chords, the first being C minor and the second E♭ major:

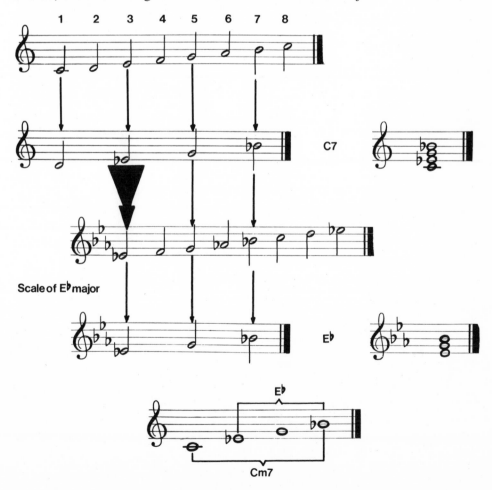

The remaining 7th chords will combine as follows:

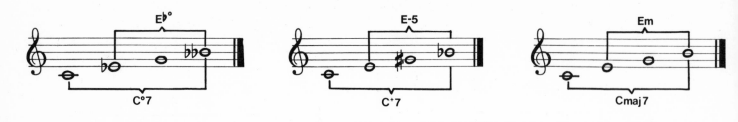

CHAPTER 30   The 9th Chord and Extended Harmonic Formulations

The 9th chord forms from a further extension of a 3rd above the dominant 7th chord. Formula $1 - 3 - 5 - \flat7 - 9$.

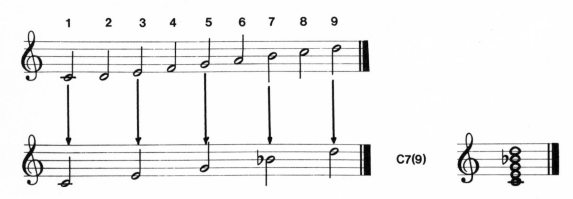

The 9th chord may also be referred to as the dominant 9th.

Further 9th chords
9th   Raise the 9th note by one semi-tone $1 - 3 - 5 - \flat7 - \sharp9$
♭9th   Lower the 9th note by one semi-tone $1 - 3 - 5 - \flat7 - \flat9$
Add 9th   Exclude the ♭7 degree, but maintain
         the 9th note to the common triad $1 - 3 - 5 - 9$

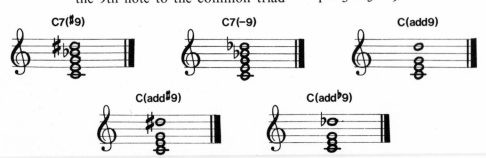

Separate chords within the 9th chord
The addition of a further 3rd above the 7th chord (within the 9th chord) allows for the dissection of at least three separate chords.

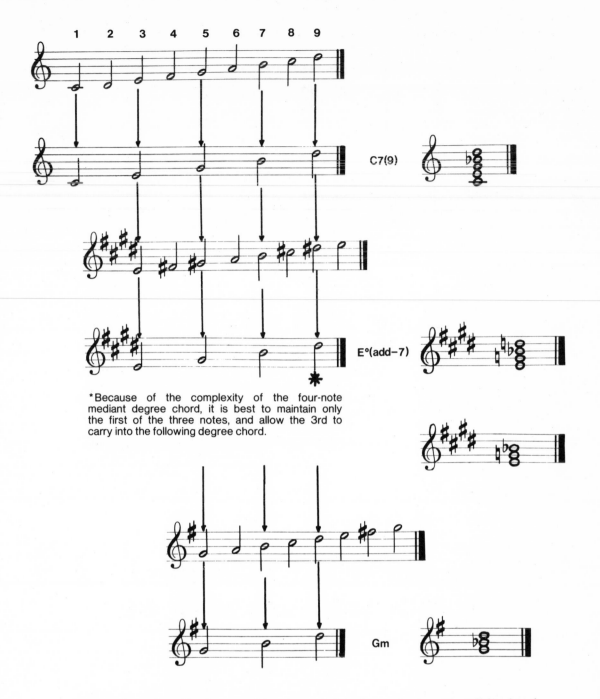

*Because of the complexity of the four-note mediant degree chord, it is best to maintain only the first of the three notes, and allow the 3rd to carry into the following degree chord.

Therefore the effective combination of chords producing the C7(9) chord are C major, E diminished and G minor:

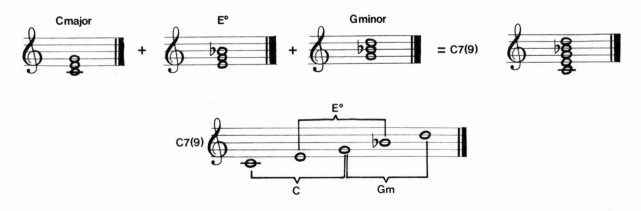

Other forms include:

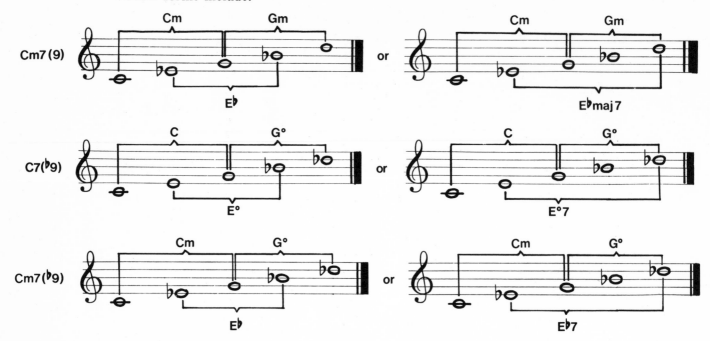

It is possible to continue this form of application until all possible combinations have been exhausted. In many cases only the three-note extensions may be correctly written since some chords will either not construct or be far too complex to name within the limited notation available.

CHAPTER 31 Combinations and Tabulations of the 11th and Suspended 4th Chords

The 11th chord
Formulate the 11th chord by a further 3rd above and including the 9th degree above the dominant 7th chord. Formula 1 – 3 – 5 – ♭7 – 9 – 11.

The 11th chord may also be referred to as the dominant 11th.

11th chord   Raise the 11th note by one semi-tone: 1 – 3 – 5 – ♭7 – 9 –11
♭11th chord   Lower the 11th note by one semi-tone: 1 – 3 – 5 – ♭7 – 9 – ♭11

Note that the 11th chord as such is not widely used. As a general rule, the suspended 4th chord (see below) is applied in lieu of the 11th with the 7th degree as required. However, if the 9th degree is to be added, the form and naming of the 11th chord must be applied. Furthermore, when applying the 11th chord, it is standard practice to omit the 5th degree due to the influence the 11th has on this note.

If the 9th degree requires alteration, this again can be amalgamated to the chord:

C7(♭9add11)   1 – 3 – 5 – ♭7 – ♭9 – 11
C7(♯9add11)   1 – 3 – 5 – ♭7 – ♯9 – 11
C7(♭9♭11)   1 – 3 – 5 – ♭7 – ♭9 – ♭11
C7(♭9♯11)   1 – 3 – 5 – ♭7 – ♭9 – ♯11
C7(♯9♭11)   1 – 3 – 5 – ♭7 – ♯9 – ♭11
C7(♯9♯11)   1 – 3 – 5 – ♭7 – ♯9 – ♯11

CHORD COMBINATIONS IN THE TABULATION
OF THE 11th CHORD

The suspended 4th chord

The suspended 4th chord is the 11th degree applied to the common chord structure. To implement the suspended 4th chord the ♭7th and 9th degrees are omitted. Formula 1 – 3 – 4(11) – 5.

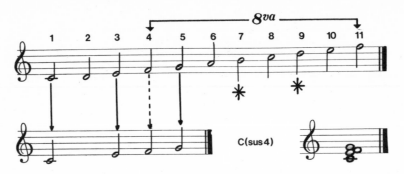

The suspended 4th may have the b7th introduced, still omitting the 9th.

C7(sus 4)   1 – 3 – 5 – ♭7 – 11(4)   or   1 – 3 – 4 – 5 – ♭7

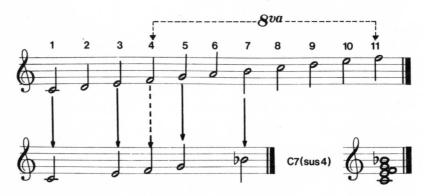

Or the 9th degree may be added without the ♭7th.

C add 9 (sus 4)   1 – 3 – 5 – 9 – 11   or   1 – 3 – 4 – 5 – 9

148

CHAPTER 32

Harmonic Relativity of the 13th and 6th Chords

The 13th chord

The 13th chord constructs with the introduction of the further 3rd above the 11th chord. Formula 1 – 3 – 5 – ♭7 – 9 – 11 – 13.

The 13th chord may also be referred to as the dominant 13th.

♯13   raise the 13th degree one semi-tone   1 – 3 – 5 – ♭7 – 9 – 11 – ♯13
♭13   lower the 13th degree one semi-tone   1 – 3 – 5 – ♭7 – 9 – 11 – ♭13

The general rule for the application of the 13th chord is to omit both the 5th and 11th degrees. Without these two scale degrees, the impact of the chord does not differ very greatly; also, if the degrees were still included, fingering of the chord would be more difficult.

It is not obligatory to omit the degrees, and many guitarists still prefer to maintain the 5th degree for certain combinations of the 11th chord.

The 5th and 11th degrees have been and will be maintained in the immediate explanations, for they are invaluable for the construction formula if the progression of the formulation of 3rds is to be maintained.

Further combinations can also be:

C7(♭9♭13)	1 – 3 – 5 – ♭7 – ♭9 – 11 – ♭13
C7(♯9♭13)	1 – 3 – 5 – ♭7 – ♯9 – 11 – ♭13
C7(♭11♭13)	1 – 3 – 5 – ♭7 – 9 – ♭11 – ♭13
C7(♯11♭13)	1 – 3 – 5 – ♭7 – 9 – ♯11 – ♭13
C7(♭9♭11♭13)	1 – 3 – 5 – ♭7 – ♭9 – ♭11 – ♭13
C7(♯9♭11♭13)	1 – 3 – 5 – ♭7 – ♯9 – ♭11 – ♭13

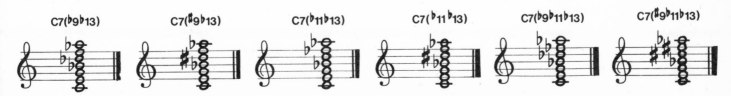

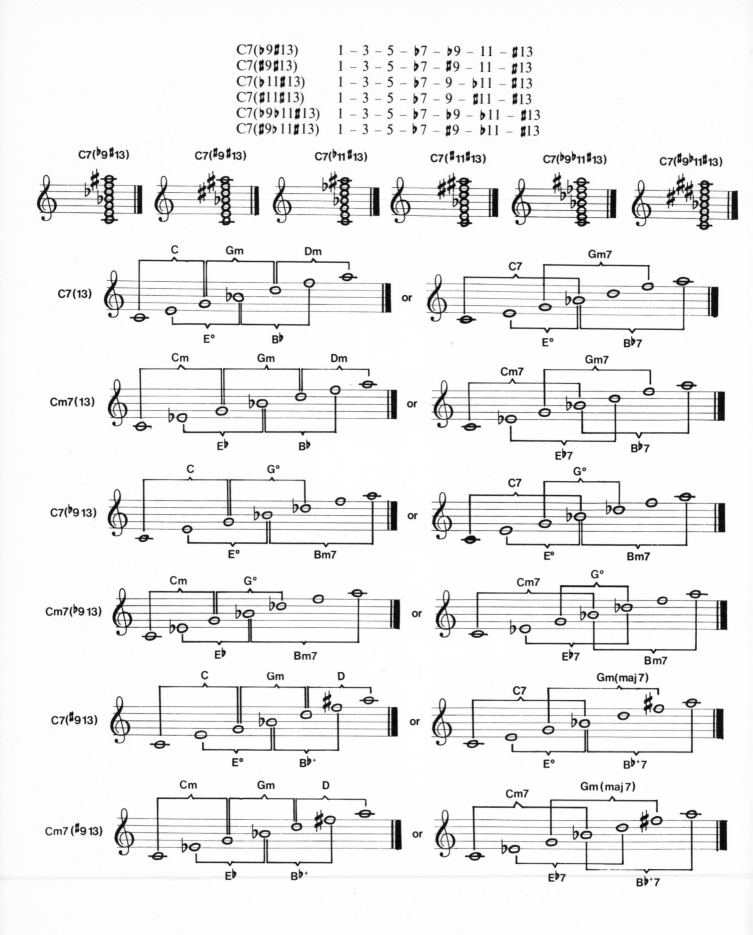

The 6th chord

The 6th chord is the 13th degree applied to the common chord structure. The 6th is applied directly to the basic triad, bypassing the ♭7th, 9th and 11th degrees. Formula 1 – 3 – 5 – 6(13).

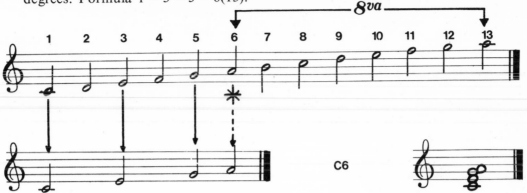

Due to its formation, the 6th chord can be written in major or minor; only the 3rd degree alters to differentiate.

Under certain circumstances the 6th degree may be lowered; this can only be applied when the 5th degree has also been lowered. In the example below, the ♭6th has been added to the diminished triad. Formula 1 – ♭3 – ♭5 – ♭6.

CHAPTER 33

The 6th (add 9th) Including the b5th Chords

Also known as the 6(9), this chord is the inclusion of the 6th degree in the common triad. The 9th degree is added without the inclusion of the b7th note. Formula 1 – 3 – 5 – 6 – 9.

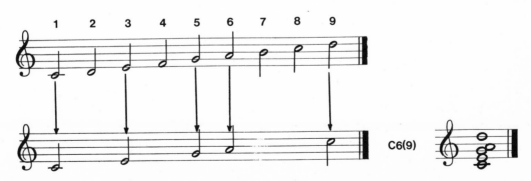

Immediately the ♭7th is included, the chord will become a dominant 9th with an added 6th (or 13th), e.g. C7(9add6) or C7(9add13).

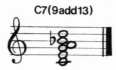

Chords with the flattened 5th degree

Chords can be written with the 5th degree lowered without becoming diminished chords. It may be necessary at times to implement the ♭5th degree, while at the same time maintaining the major 3rd degree. Formula 1 – 3 – ♭5.

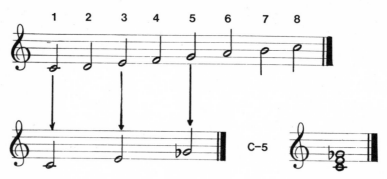

Although the chord may be used on its own, it is more commonly used with a dominant or extended chord.

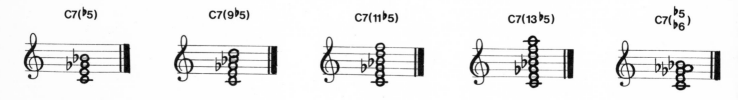

CHAPTER 34

Review of the Basic Fundamentals of Chord Construction

Chords construct from the major scale by the continuance of 3rds.

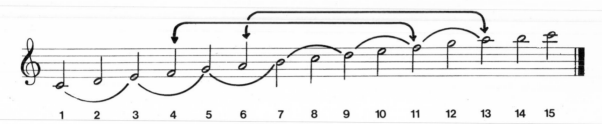

All chords basically extend into and follow on from one chord to another. An omission of a note, or a series of notes, will alter the chord name. Similarly, if a degree structure is altered, this will also change the immediate name of the chord.

The principal placement of the interval must at all times be employed to determine the formation of the chord.

The basic structures and applications of chords are set out below. These may be altered and added to as required, realising that the interval still governs the chord.

MAJOR	1 – 3 – 5	major 3rd degree
MINOR	1 – ♭3 – 5	minor 3rd degree
7th (dominant)	1 – 3 – 5 – ♭7	basis of extensions
9th (dominant)	1 – 3 – 5 – ♭7 – 9	succession of 3rds above ♭7th
add 9th	1 – 3 – 5 – 9	succession of 3rds omitting ♭7th
11th (dominant)	1 – 3 – 5 – ♭7 – 9 – 11	succession of 3rds above 9th
sus 4th	1 – 3 – 4 – 5	11th note returned one octave against common triad (4)
13th	1 – 3 – 5 – ♭7 – 9 –11 – 13	succession of 3rds above 11th 13th note returned one octave
6th	1 – 3 – 5 – 6	against common triad (6)
6/9	1 – 3 – 5 – 6 – ♭7 – 9	13th chord applied without 11th; 13th degree returned one octave against common triad (6)
6 add 9th	1 – 3 – 5 – 6 – 9	13th chord omitting the 11th and ♭7th
AUGMENTED	1 – 3 – ♯5	augmented 5th degree; major 3rds
AUGMENTED 7th	1 – 3 – ♯5 – ♭7	augmented 5th degree including ♭7th note; succession in major 3rds to minor 3rd
DIMINISHED	1 – ♭3 – ♭5	minor 3rd and diminished 5th degrees; succession in minor 3rds
DIMINISHED 7th	1 – ♭3 – ♭5 – ♭♭7	expanded succession of minor 3rds
b5 chord	1 – 3 – ♭5	major 3rd to diminished 3rd
7th b5th	1 – 3 – ♭5 – ♭7	dominant 7th with diminished 3rd (3 to b5)

SUPPLEMENT A

Blues and 12-bar playing

SECTION 1

A Brief History of the Blues

Blues belong traditionally to the American Negro and originated in the southern part of the USA. The style and syncopated rhythmic patterns of blues can be traced back to the 1860s, although music of this characteristic pattern can be dated as far back as 1834 through pieces such as 'Turkey in the Straw' and 'Old Zip Coony'.

Religion played an important part in blues development. Preachers, in the course of their sermons, often passed from ordinary speech to emotional outbursts with an informalised notation approaching singing.

Many have tried to isolate the characteristic form of the blues solo; and it has at times been linked in style to the current music of India, Arabia, Spain, Africa (the original home of the Negro), the Caribbean and, more recently, New Orleans. However, it constantly changes in style and form, with only the pattern of the rhythmic structure remaining unaltered.

Commercial entertainment has dictatorially set rules for three of the most common forms—8 bars, 12 bars and 16 bars—from which the 12-bar pattern has emerged as victor in terms of the form blues should take.

Melody is characteristic of 'blues notes'. They are quite often employed by the musician (constantly seemingly out of musical character) who, as a soloist, continually seems to play different material although it is structurally 'basic and unaltered'.

Another characteristic of blues is that it is played by the individual *with the feeling and character of that individual;* but the rhythmic pattern, *not* the solo performer, sets the style of the music.

At one time it was thought that blues might provide a style of performance in the orthodox European tradition, but this has constantly proven to be a mistaken idea—in fact, blues is a form of American gypsy music.

The peculiar rhythmic pattern of blues is one that can easily change with, and adjust to, musical evolution. Its pattern of rhythm has an almost 'primitive' animal character with which each 'younger generation', as an idealistic audience, can readily identify.

As the environment of modern life changes, so does the style of blues playing. Although the different generations listen to basically the same form of music (played on different groups of instruments) a definite 'music generation gap' always exists.

Throughout the twentieth century the principle of 12-bar blues has remained constant—further proof of the need to fulfill the 'primitive' instincts of younger people, as the following chronological analysis quite explicitly shows.

(a) The early 1910s saw the introduction of Jazz, a traditionally spontaneous breakaway from the alternate style of blues. This decade saw in 1917 the beginning of the revolutionary 'Basin Street Blues'.

(b) Music of the 1920s introduced the sound of the Charleston, one of the first commercially induced 'hysterical' types of music.

(c) The 'Big Band' era evolved in the 1930s, and was also based on the formula of the traditional blues.

(d) The 1940s period saw the rise of 'Cool' and 'Bop' music. Involved vocal and instrumental harmonisation was at its most pleasant peak commercially. The period also saw the development of the 'combo' bands and arrangements that are still popular with bands today.

(e) Rock & Roll began in the mid-1950s, at a time when the 'Boogie' mode had taken the world by storm; both of these forms were based on the traditional 12-bar blues style.

(f) The 1960s saw a much more sophisticated form of the 12-bar blues pattern, but with the same basic characteristics as that of the previous decade. At this time the first of the commercial electronic sounds developed—high-pitched electric guitars relying on heavy echo sounds for effect.

(g) The 1970s continued with the blues format—but a format that was induced electronically and expressed much more freely. More rules have been broken (in the traditional solo sense), but the basic 12-bar blues pattern still remains, though it is enhanced by a more articulate form (including more volume) of electric bass guitar playing.

SECTION 2
Playing 12-bar Blues

One of the most widely used forms of 12-bar blues playing (and also one of the most acceptable) is the style known as 4 – 2 – 1.

The 4 – 2 – 1 style is in no way related to the interval or tonal progressions of the music concerned. In fact, it relates only to the structure of the bars in music.

If the standard key form of tonic, sub-dominant and dominant chords were taken into account in this style, only their placement within bars would be applied. The system is:

4 BARS	TONIC CHORD
2 BARS	SUB-DOMINANT CHORD
2 BARS	TONIC CHORD
1 BAR	DOMINANT CHORD
1 BAR	SUB-DOMINANT CHORD
1 BAR	TONIC CHORD
1 BAR	DOMINANT CHORD
12 BARS	TOTAL

Note that this progression relates only to repetitive playing. The final playing of the system should have the twelfth bar as the tonic chord. This final twelfth bar tonic is applied to end effectively the form of the music on its key note.

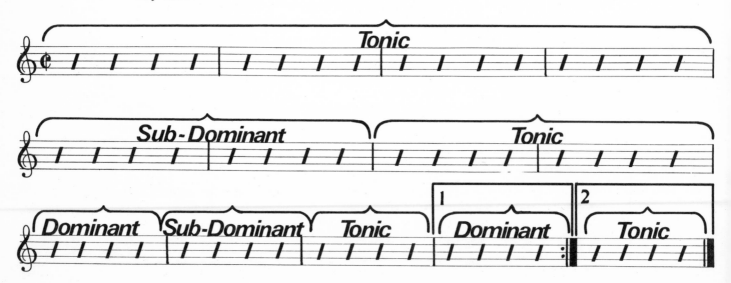

If this 12-bar structure were applied to the key of F major it would produce these chords:

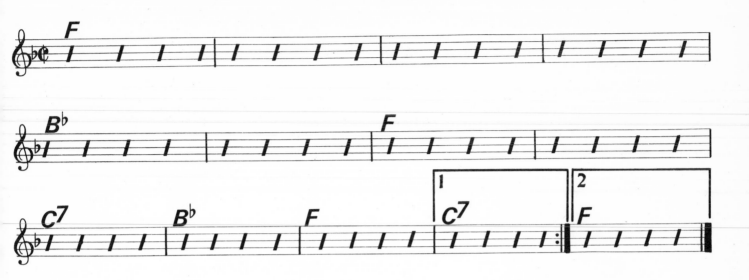

KEY OF F MAJOR

TONIC	F MAJOR
SUB-DOMINANT	Bb MAJOR
DOMINANT	C7th

The key of F major has been selected because it is the most common key used for the playing of 12-bar blues in a moveable pattern.

All chords of the F major key can be located within the first position, and can be moved to any selected position (changing the key of the pattern) while at the same time maintaining the identical chord and pattern sequence with minimal effort.

The tonic and sub-dominant chords are of the barré form, and make for ease of finger interchange, whereas the dominant chord (although not of the barré style) causes a 'chunky' effect with the deadened first and sixth strings.

By using the 'moveable key of the F major combination' it is possible for the beginner to play in ten standard major key 12-bar blues progressions with minimal effort. In each case the fingers are maintained in only one position for the full performance.

The following table may now be used for all of the stated keys, simply by following the 4 – 2 – 1 formula and selecting the required key from the chart together with the relevant chord fingering.

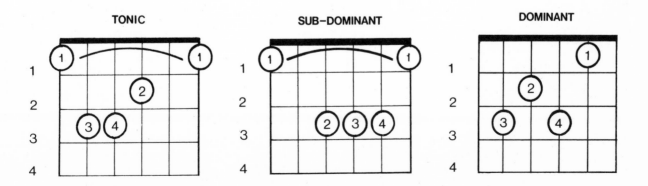

FRET	KEY OF	Tonic chord	Sub-dominant chord	Dominant chord
1	F	F	B♭	C7
2	F♯	F♯	B	C♯7
	G♭	G♭	C♭	D♭7
3	G	G	C	D7
4	✻ G♯	G♯	C♯	D♯7
	A♭	A♭	D♭	E♭7
5	A	A	D	E7
6	✻ A♯	A♯	D♯	E♯7
	B♭	B♭	E♭	F7
7	B	B	E	F♯7
	C♭	C♭	F♭	G♭7
8	C	C	F	G7

* Chords rarely used in major, but will be of value
to the student when applying minor forms.

The following is an example of the same blues music pattern used in the key of G major, by the application of the immediate arpeggio and based on the chord degrees 1 – 3 – 5 – 3 (tonic – mediant – dominant – mediant).

Within the key of G major the chords are G, C and D7th respectively. This same pattern can also be used in the moveable format (see the F major moveable form, page   ) and can also be played as a Rock & Roll or blues solo.

The total movement of notational forms in this format allows for constant variation within the same scope of chordal structures. So long as the original 4 – 2 – 1 style is maintained, variant forms are possible.

Boogie style 12-bar blues: One such form is the Boogie style (very popular in modern Rock & Roll) which relies on movements of semi-tones (ascending and descending) between the 3rd and 5th degrees of the chord in use.

Although the Boogie style offers little change from the blues examples previously shown, it is open to interpretation. It can either be played in the present style, or may be written in quaver form, allowing each of the two bars to be played as one. This allows the music to be effectively doubled in its total playable length without having to change the original structure.

As shown in the original example, the solo form can be interchanged, as desired, by the individual.

Another of the more common blues styles is the crotchet – quaver – quaver – crotchet – quaver – quaver per bar rhythm.

Further effects are gained through the slide approach. This is done by playing the note of the minor 3rd and sliding the finger concerned to the major 3rd degree. This style is called the *gliss* movement.

To complete the form, the major 6th degree is added above the 5th, and there is then a return to the 5th degree in the second half bar, which is generally of total quaver extraction.

Although commonly used, the gliss style has far too many variants to be shown within the limited space available.

Remember that interpretations of this nature (no matter how commonly used) are personal and, although they are based on formulae, strict adherence is not obligatory.

A further moveable form can also be found in the key of B♭.

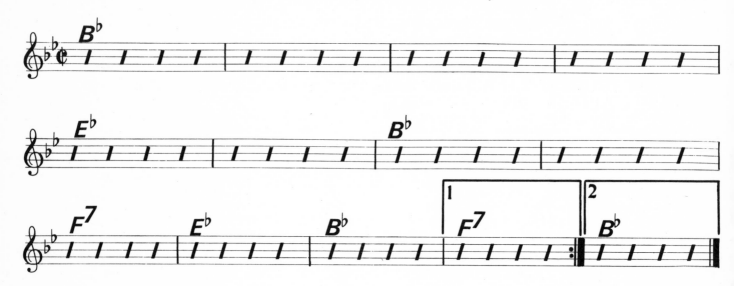

KEY OF B♭ MAJOR

TONIC	B♭ MAJOR
SUB-DOMINANT	E♭ MAJOR
DOMINANT	F7th

The above pattern is also moveable in the same manner as the F major formation (offering a similar number of keys) while at the same time completing the compass of the chromatic key.

The main difference between the two alternate forms is that the sub-dominant chord is two frets above the other chords of the same key.

TONIC SUB–DOMINANT DOMINANT

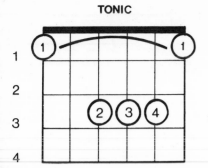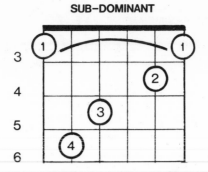

FRET	KEY OF	Tonic chord	Sub-dominant chord	Dominant chord
1	✻ A♯	A♯	D♯	E♯7
	B♭	B♭	E♭	F7
2	B	B	E	F♯7
	C♭	C♭	F♭	G♭7
3	C	C	F	G7
4	C♯	C♯	F♯	G♯7
	D♭	D♭	G♭	A♭7
5	D	D	G	A7
6	✻ D♯	D♯	G♯	A♯7
	E♭	E♭	A♭	B♭7
7	E	E	A	B7
8	F	F	B♭	C7

* Chords rarely used in major, but will be of value to
the student when applying minor forms.

The less common form of 12-bar applications is the 1 – 1 – 2 – 2 – 2 – 1 – 1 – 2 series. The system is:

TONIC CHORD	1 BAR
SUB-DOMINANT CHORD	1 BAR
TONIC CHORD	2 BARS
SUB-DOMINANT CHORD	2 BARS
TONIC CHORD	2 BARS
DOMINANT CHORD	1 BAR
SUB-DOMINANT CHORD	1 BAR
TONIC CHORD	2 BARS
TOTAL	12 BARS

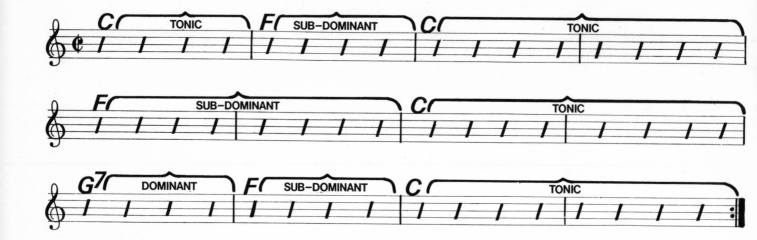

SECTION 3
Rhythmic Patterns and Effects

Alternate chord rhythmic forms can also be:

Or, the two types can be joined together to form alternate bar rhythmic patterns within the one 12-bar structure.

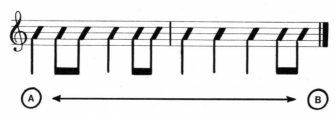

Special effects: Effects used in the playing of chords almost invariably make, or break, the style being sought. For this reason each should be studied carefully and applied as stated.

Deadened chords: The effect is manufactured by not fully pressurising the chord concerned, producing a 'chunky' sound.

Staccato chords: Raise the fingers off the chord immediately it is fully sounded. The sound immediately following can be likened to a deadened chord.

Accent: Used in the same way as conventional music forms. Strike the chord much harder than the other beats surrounding it.

Note that all three of these effects can be used, in any combination desired, at the one time, e.g.:

Rests: May also be used within the beats of a bar. The heel of the right hand should be placed against the strings to obtain the total area of silence required.

SECTION 4
Combined 7th Chord and Additional Effects

An alternate form of the combined 12-bar patterns studied to date is the use of the combined form of 1 – 1 – 2 (etc.) and the 4 – 2 – 1 systems, applying the last bar of the 4 – 2 – 1 series as a 7th chord.

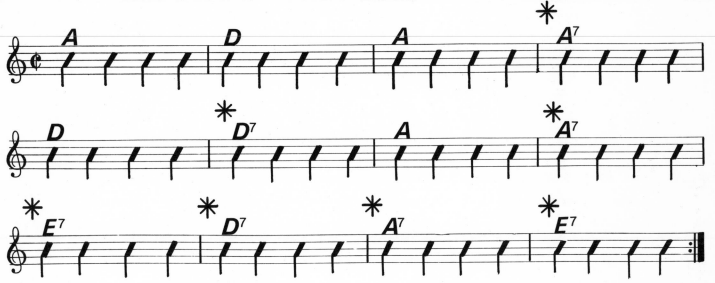

These additional forms of the 7th chords are required for the introduction of the tonic and sub-dominant chords in the combined pattern style.

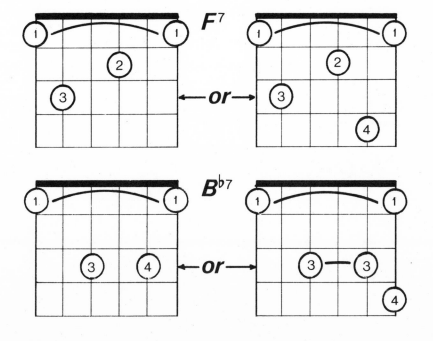

Additional interchangeable rhythmic patterns include:

SECTION 5
The Turn-Around and Optional Effects

The turn-around is a form of 12-bar playing developed in the late 1950s which still enjoys immense popularity today.

'Turn-around' songs are quite frequently played slowly, although they have a feeling of speed in their final application.

This form of music has one more chord than those of the standard key pattern. It is usually the relative to the tonic chord.

Each chord is played at one-bar intervals and the dominant chord is sometimes applied without the 7th degree.

The turn-around is more commonly played in triplet form:

Other variations on the triplet bars are:

SECTION 6
Moveable Blues and Advanced Expression

Among the more modern forms of 12-bar blues playing, additive chords are used to create a 'walking' effect in the production of rhythm.

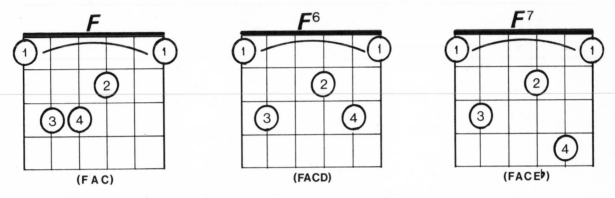

Apart from the additional colour these chords create, they also allow the bass player to produce a far more pronounced form of alternate backing.

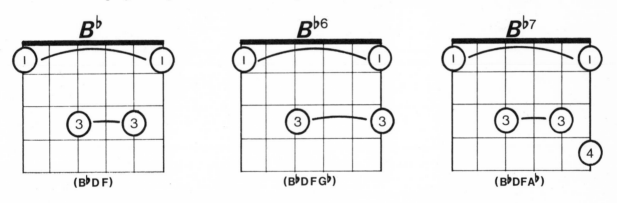

The style to which these chords are applied is the original 12-bar style discussed on pages 156-158.

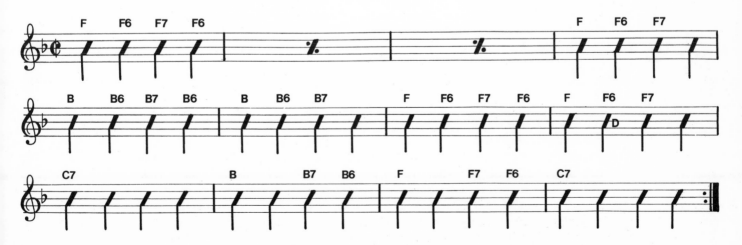

165

Further rhythms of advanced expression forms include:

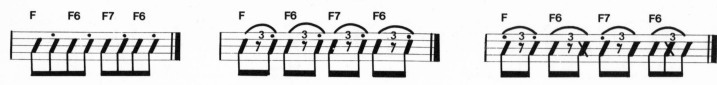

Additional rock expression:

SECTION 7
The Application of Jazz Blues

Jazz blues can be applied to the turn-around. The basic difference between the standard turn-around and the Jazz blues is that the latter uses expanded chord rather than the strict major or minor patterns.

In the immediate transition, the chords alter as follows:

MAJOR CHORDS become MAJOR 7th CHORDS
MINOR CHORDS become MINOR 7th CHORDS
DOMINANT 7th become DOMINANT 9th CHORDS

THE MODERN ALTERNATE BLUES FORM

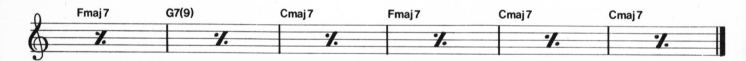

SECTION 8
The Slide Chord

Chords of the 12-bar pattern can be enhanced by a semi-tone lowering of the last beat of each bar (or when the performer so desires) in the original 12-bar cycle.

It is suggested that this form of application be restricted to a minimum; prolonged playing could tend to disharmonise and ruin the effect sought at any given time. But, used correctly, it could become one of the greatest assets within the scope of the 12-bar framework.

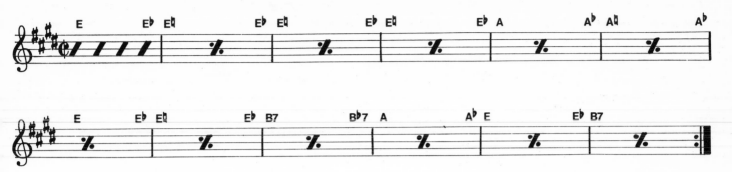

SECTION 9
Solo Blues and Boogies

This is another style of blues progression relying quite heavily on the application of the 7th degree in repetitious form before returning to the 5th degree through the 6th.

The first of these examples shows the 7th applied prior to the third bar beat, whereas the following one applies the 7th degree on the third beat. To achieve this the first beat is a doubled tonic note.

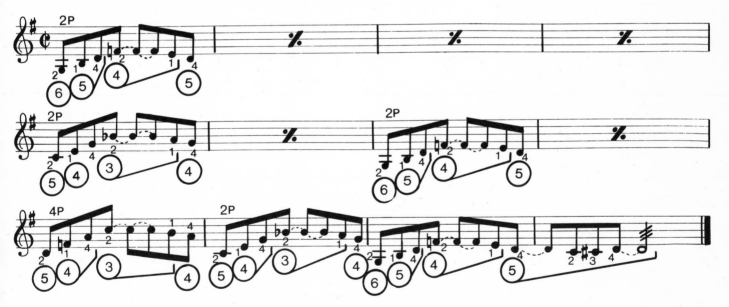

The previous example has been shown in the second position, with the only exception being the dominant chord which, although maintaining the same pattern, is played two frets higher (or, two positions higher).

These examples (and all of the others within this blues supplement) can be applied with the moveable format application: begin each example in the third position for the key of A♭; begin in the fourth position for the key of A; begin in the fifth position for the key of B♭; etc.

SECTION 10
Blues Improvising

Although the style of each performer may alter in his application of certain improvising patterns, most musicians will agree that the most common form of improvising is the application of the minor 7th, suspended 4th — M7 (sus 4) — arpeggio.

The arpeggio is played (at the performer's interpretation) by the use of the minor 7th (sus 4th) chord against the major chord in use against the blues pattern.

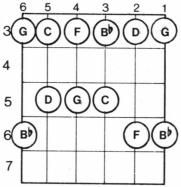

One of the most common teaching methods is based on the construction of this particular arpeggio in the third position against the G major chord.

The Gm7 (sus 4) — G – B♭ – C – D – F — can be fingered in the manner shown without altering the character of the chord in the one position (being the third position) and each note is played in a combination peculiar to the individual guitarist.

Blues improvising will be totally ineffective without syncopating each cluster of preferred notation. The example shown below is only a guide, and there is no obligation to adhere to this form of performance.

The following table shows the range of notes available within the fifteen-fret area, applying this particular blues form. Note that it is possible to produce a series of positions within the systematic form. The formula may also be maintained while the chord sequence may modulate (transpose) to any other key, higher or lower, than the arpeggio shown here.

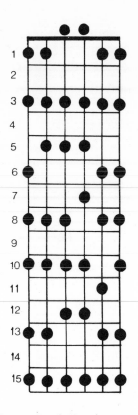

A closer study will show the following positions forming:

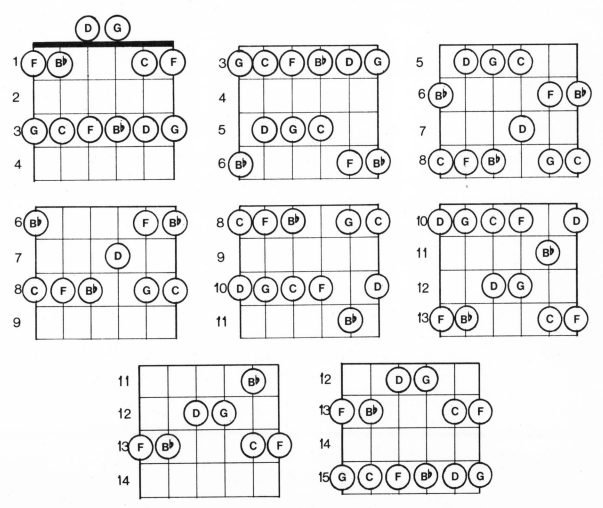

These positions allow for continual change (of position) within the one chord. Remember, although notation may be at the same unison pitch at an alternate position, it will have a totally different colour.

Hammer blows (ascending slurs): Hammer blows are usually applied between the flattened 3rd and the 4th degrees. This adds one additional note (the major 3rd) and is played by striking only the first note and then hammering the remaining two notes. B♭ – B♮ – C.

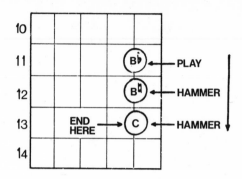

The twist is usually applied to the 4th degree, which is either rolled upwards or pulled downwards to duplicate the sound of the 5th degree (twist C until the D note is heard).

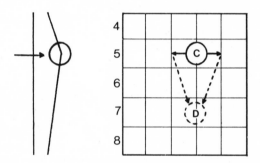

Reverse hammer blows (descending slurs) are applied by beginning at the 8th (upper tonic) degree and sliding the fingers through the major 7th note to end on the minor 7th note (b7th). As with the hammer blow, only the first of the three notes is plucked. The final two are sounded by pulling off the neck with the left-hand fingers. G – F♯ – F♮.

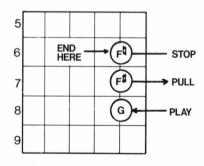

170

SUPPLEMENT B
Transposition Chart

Many new players have continual trouble transposing music from one key to another. In many cases it has caused hours of fruitless work because of a lack of knowledge of the scale forms, or because they are not fully aware of how to transpose the music to a more suitable key even with correct understanding.

To facilitate progress (while your knowledge improves) and to cut down on the frustrations of incorrect transposition, the following Transposition Table has been formulated.

You will now only have to look at the key signature, irrespective of whether the key is of its major or its relative minor, and transpose to the key (by the most suitable key signature shown) to the one desired.

Not only can each note be transposed to the required key (simply by replacement of position with the new key signature), but all chord symbols can also be changed by the same system, maintaining the structure of the chord symbol and only altering its name.

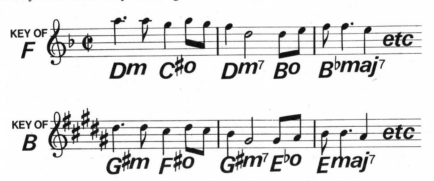

Any accidentals applied to the original score are also transposed by direct replacement; or, if these clash with the new key signature, changes can be made by the substitution of new accidentals.

Throughout the transpositions the range of the interval of any scale note, from its new tonic note, will remain unaltered. It is incorrect to substitute with enharmonic notes. If the transposed notes (of the new key signature) become too complex, apply the enharmonic key.

KEY OF	1	2	3	4	5	6	7	8
C	C	D	E	F	G	A	B	C
C♯	C♯	D♯	E♯	F♯	G♯	A♯	B♯	C♯
D♭	D♭	E♭	F	G♭	A♭	B♭	C	D♭
D	D	E	F♯	G	A	B	C♯	D
E♭	E♭	F	G	A♭	B♭	C	D	E♭
E	E	F♯	G♯	A	B	C♯	D♯	E
F	F	G	A	B♭	C	D	E	F
F♯	F♯	G♯	A♯	B	C♯	D♯	E♯	F♯
G♭	G♭	A♭	B♭	C♭	D♭	E♭	F	G♭
G	G	A	B	C	D	E	F♯	G
A♭	A♭	B♭	C	D	E♭	F	G	A♭
A	A	B	C♯	D	E	F♯	G♯	A
B♭	B♭	C	D	E♭	F	G	A	B♭
B	B	C♯	D♯	E	F♯	G♯	A♯	B
C♭	C♭	D♭	E♭	F♭	G♭	A♭	B♭	C♭
C	C	D	E	F	G	A	B	C
KEY OF	1	2	3	4	5	6	7	8

Index

174

Index — Musical Content (Songs)

176